Profitable Trading Strategy

3 Candle and 4 Candle Play

By Rashid Rehman

Table of Contents

Why learn this Strategy

This is a momentum based, high probability and profitable strategy like my other trading strategies. After training, mentoring and working with hedge fund managers and institution traders, I decided to help the trading community by splitting the cost of stock market trading education. By writing single strategy, I can concentrate on the quality, it's also helps break the cost down.

As stated by a wise person ''Keep learning from birth to the last breath. I also like the saying that every living being is either dying every moment or growing, a person who learn and grow is definitely going towards more living. Hey, you are for sure going towards life. With that in mind, learning and development is very important for an individual to grow.

Stock trading is not different than any other businesses out there. Trading needs capital, a trading plan, time, a contingency plan and high probability strategies. For trading to be a successful business one would need to keep learning and adding new tools and techniques to their tool box.

Also, finding this profitable candlestick price-pattern does not require programming your scanner or pay monthly subscription fee for a scanner, I have explained in detail what to look for and how to find the pattern along with time of day, setting up your charts etc. Obviously, a scanner can be programmed to find these patterns if you already have access to one.

The other most important aspect of this price pattern is that this profitable pattern is traded by hedge funds, banks and other professional traders i.e. the Smart Money. When a trader utilizes this strategy, they are trading in synch with the smart money.

To be honest and clear, this strategy book is not a biography neither has any entertaining stories; this is a true stock trading strategy you can learn and apply to financial markets and make money. My humble intentions are to help you learn more about stock trading with less money and in short period.

Benefits of price pattern

In the world of stock trading, I have seen individuals and institutions use different strategies based on a range of factors and indicators. They all have one parameter in common i.e. the price, and all their actions and behaviors move the price in certain ways. As we human are creature of habits, our actions in certain situations are predictable.

The 3 candle play explained in this book is due to human habits, emotions and actions they take in excitement and fear.

The benefits of trading of a fixed price pattern (combination of candles) is that a pattern gives us an optimal entry. We know our exit when we are wrong and most importantly, we know how to manage in between the entry and exit, which I have explained in detail. In between management is something our trading results (profits) depends on.

During this strategy package I will teach how to recognize the pattern, the time frames to watch, when to enter, how to manage while in trade and obviously the exit. A known price pattern is like seeing a friend in a crowded street where you don't have to think about his name, address etc as you know all the information. Similarly knowing particular patterns and associated strategies, enable us to straightaway know where to enter, how to manage and exit the trade.

You will also need to know

I will dive a bit deeper than the law of supply and demand. All stocks move in four major phases, (like lunar phases→ Joking). For real, stocks have phases of accumulation, demand, distribution and supply.

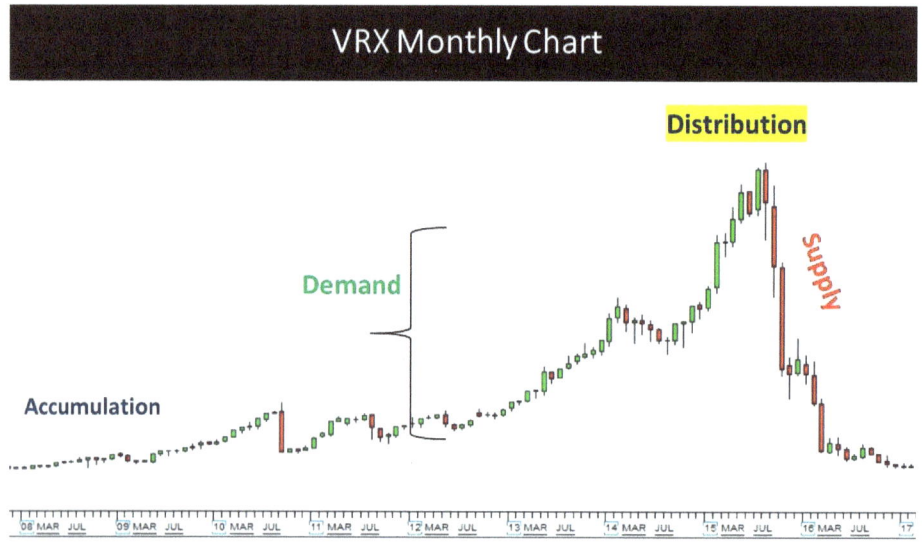

The accumulation phase is a low volume, narrow bars, dead stock no one believes will move. Then one day the unexpected happens and stock come out of that narrow range low volume base on relatively high volume. After slight pullback, the stock starts moving up and the 2nd phase starts. 2nd phase (demand) is driven by the emotion of greed; the stock goes up to new highs, some buys, other watch the move.

Third phase is the distribution where we notice all the good news about the company. 3rd phase is very late to buy. After the good news and upgrades from analysts, general interest increases in the stock, hence the volume and candle size also start increasing, followed by a few false breakouts. These are all the symptoms of top forming. If you are a stock specialist, you will notice the end of the move and will only look to short rather than long the stock. When stock start moving down, stock enters its fourth phase know as bearish market. In bearish market stocks move down very quickly due to more supply. This fourth phase is driven by the emotion of fear. After the fourth phase, stock enters its 1st phase and then the whole process starts again.

Other than the stock phases, it would be good to know and understand candle stick charts, moving averages, trading and investment basics and more importantly knowing one's own emotions. Knowing self is better than every strategy book available in the market.

The Pattern:

An extremely powerful trading **setup** that can be seen in all time frames during the day. This **pattern** works on the principle of push–rest– push. When the market opens, the stock price moves up (the push) making a decent size green candle, on a relatively high volume. Then price stays in a **narrow range** (the rest) forming a **narrow bar**, where the narrow bar should stay in the top 50% of first bar, followed by another push in the direction of the initial move. The move continues towards new highs until **toping signs** or price reaches the **target**. This pattern is based on momentum and has the profit potential of multiple Risk units.

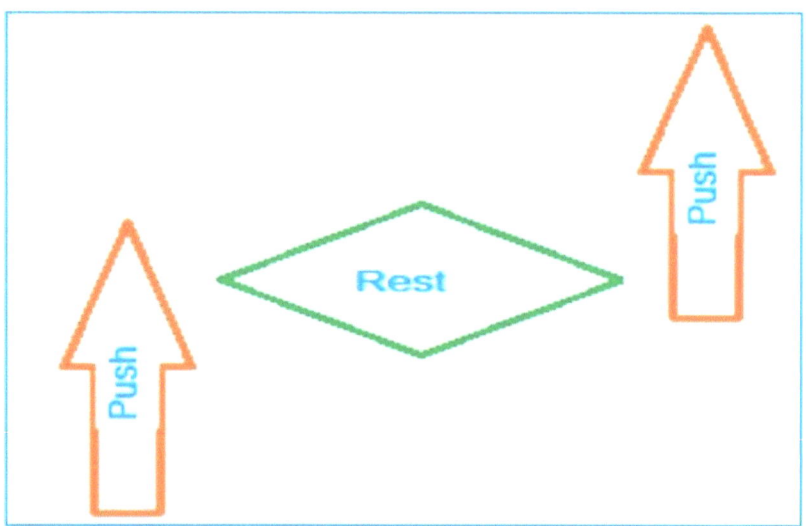

The Psychology Behind the Pattern

Every price movement in the stock market is the result of human behavior (trading algos are also designed by humans). The reason behind a move in the market is also known as the psychology of the mass. To apply the psychology of the mass to this pattern, I will divide different opinions into groups.

The initial up push during the formation of this pattern creates an excitement in the group who were fully bullish. Another middle-minded group says ''let's watch and see what happens next''. The bearish group with no position is excited and looking for opportunities to short. Another bearish group which is already short (and the water is coming up to their neck), start hoping and praying for the price to come back down, whilst some traders will be looking to add to their short position. Hey what's the pro traders doing at this stage... shshshhhhh. Actually, Professional traders are waiting, as one green bar is an incomplete picture and professionals don't waste their capital and energy on low odd plays. Professionals will normally wait for the pattern to complete.

Hmmmmm......... Isn't it getting a bit spicy just with one green candle, holy Fish. With the narrow bar forming the bullish group buys the stock. The other neutral bullish group is still not clear.

The bearish group, which was looking for higher price to short, sees the price halting as a sign of weakness and starts shorting the stock. The already short bearish group adds to their position to reduce their average price. So, what's happening at this stage..........? A pressure under the surface has developed and the ground is shaking, ready to explode.

Guess where the bearish groups are putting their stop loss? Interestingly, over the highs of the initial green bar and the narrow bar. Surely there will be a panic above the highs of these two bars and that's where professional elite traders come into play.

Experienced traders buy above the highs and put stop below the narrow bar.

Now recall the old guru's first lesson about supply and demand and think how many groups are buying above the highs of bar 1 and 2 (see figure below), the experienced traders, the bearish traders who just short the stock and the bearish group who were already short. The group which has added to their short position, got no way except to buy and cover their position because they already knew they were wrong and with adding more their losses got more worse.

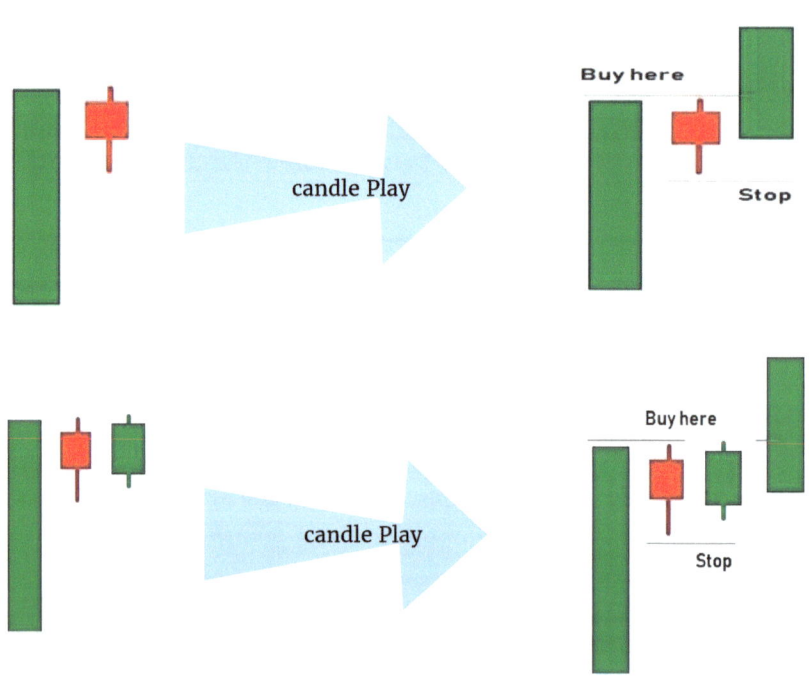

I am sure you have always wondered who buys at the top. Remember there was one group who were bullish but not sure, when they see the price going up and up and up again, they cannot tolerate any further upside move, their brain is screaming "Told you it's going up, buy-buy-buy", the time they finally buys, you can notice high volume and a comparatively wide range bar which usually ends the up move.

Enough about the pattern and the mojo which form the pattern, lets derive a true trading strategy of this price pattern:

As shown above in the 3 candle play, the first bar is a wide range green bar clearing some resistance and goes up to a key area. The key area could be a half or whole number, previous day close or a moving average on daily chart. The narrow range bar (the rest) is basically accumulation under that key area and the entry bar (3rd bar) goes through that key area and proceeds to new highs.

In some instances when the key area is stronger, the stock form two narrow bars after the 1st bar, this is called the 4 candle play, where the entry bar is the 4th bar clearing the key area and moving to new highs.

The Strategy

By now you should know that pattern is how price moves and which human emotions drive them. A price pattern without a strategy is like a powerful vehicle without fuel. Without any further delay, lets load our vehicle with the appropriate fuel and move on:

Time Frames to watch

Professional traders get into a position when multiple time frame aligns i.e. to go long on a bullish daily chart, the pro traders will only enter a position once the lower time frame starts trending higher. To achieve multiple time frames alignment, professional traders watch time frames as mentioned below:

During the opening market:

❖ Time frames to watch are daily chart, 1min, 2min and 5min charts.
❖ At 10:00am (NY time) you should be watching Daily, 2min, 5min and 15min
❖ After 10:30am to market close you can watch Daily, 5min, 15min and 60min charts

Finding the pattern

Time (from –to) (EST)	Time Frame to watch	Pattern to look for
09:30 – 09:32 am	1 min	3 candle play
09:30 – 09:33 am	1min	4 candle play
09:32 – 09:34 am	2min	3 candle play
09:34 – 09:36 am	2min	4 candle play
09:38 – 09:45 am	5min	3 candle play
09:45 – 09:50 am	5min	4 candle play
09:50 – 10:00 am	15min	3 candle play
10:00– 10:15 am	15min	4 candle play
After 11:30	60 min	3 candle play

Pattern Requirements

Daily

A very clear up trend, above 20 /50/200 moving average or coming up of a double bottom. And most importantly have room to move up with no overhead resistance. A clear catalyst, bear traps, good news with high short interest etc.

Trade Management

The key to trading success is to enter a position when all the following requirement aligns:

1- The Daily is a clear bullish
2- There is no overhead immediate resistance and room to move higher
3- Enter only when the entry management requirements are met
4- Manage as per the strategy once in the trade.
5- Exit as per exit management

During the day trade, you can manage trades with the following three methods.

Entry Management

3 Candle Play

First bar: A wide or mid-range green bar moves up to a key level, resistance area, a whole or half number forming a significant area. First bar usually has high volume.
2nd bar: A narrow bar in the upper 50% of the 1st bar.

❖ First and 2nd bar have almost equal highs where 2nd bar is formed in the top 50% of 1st bar.

Entry: Buy above the high of first and second bars

Stop: Put your stop below the low of narrow bar, obviously two to three cents below not to the exact penny.

4 Candle Play

First Bar: A wide or mid-range green bar moves up to a key level, resistance area, a whole or half number forming a significant area. First bar usually has high volume.

2nd & 3rd Bars: Narrow bars in upper 50% of the 1st bar.

❖ First, 2nd and 3rd bars have almost equal highs where 2nd and 3rd bar is formed in the top 50% of 1st bar.

Entry: Buy above the high of first, second and third bars

Stop: Put your stop below the low of narrow 2nd or 3rd candle(whichever is lower). Obviously two to three cents below not to the exact penny.

In trade management:

This strategy requires basic trade management, which is, not to take any action as long as the price remains above the stop.

In-trade management applies the same way to both 3 candle play and 4 candle play.

Exit Management:

2R- AON: (wait- let me explain); 2R-AON is two risk unit on all position or nothing, which means if you are risking $100 per trade you will exit all position when the profit reaches to $200 else you will take a stop loss.

AON: (you got it); All or nothing is an aggressive exit management strategy where the trader have a pre-determined target. The trader in this case is sure that price in a certain scenario moves to x point so they wait till price reaches that point or take a stop loss. For example: buy near pivot point and sell All on R1/R2 or take a stop.

BBB: (what...) OK OK; BBB is Bar by Bar management for example you entered a trade in a 3 candle play using one minute chart (third bar is entry bar), once third bar completes and fourth bar starts you move the stop under 3rd bar, once fourth bar completes and fifth starts you move the stop under fourth bar and so on, to the point when your stop taken out or target reached.

Moving Average: Once your trade triggers you stay in the trade as long as the price remains above a moving average, you can use 8, 9 or 20ema for this type of management.

Combo management: Trade can also be exited by combining some of the above exit management. Eg one known way is to exit ¾ position once profit reached to 2R and manage the rest bar by bar, AON or exit end of the day.

Share Sizing

- ❖ Your share size is based on your risk amount (R) divided by your stop:
- ❖ Share Size = Risk / Size of Stop

Example 1: Risk "R" per trade is $500 | Entry: $22.45 | Stop $21.95
- ❖ Stop loss: $22.45 – $21.95 = $0.50
- ❖ Number of shares: $500 / $0.50 = 1,000 shares

Example 2: Risk "R" per trade is $50 | Entry: $22.45 | Stop $21.95
- ❖ Stop loss: $22.45 – $21.95 = $0.50
- ❖ Number of shares: $50 / $0.50 = 100 shares

Risk 'R' is the amount you risk per trade and the intentions on every trade is to make multiple of Risk amount. For example, if risk $500 per trade, your aim would be making $1000, $1500 or more per trade.

Risk Disclaimer:

Please read US Security and Exchange commission investor publication regarding risk associated with all types of financial markets. Click here Or use the link below:

https://www.sec.gov/reportspubs/investor-publications/investorpubsdaytipshtm.html

Example Charts

The moving averages I used are as follows: You are not required to have moving averages on your chart for this strategy. On intraday time frames I have 20 ema, 9 ema and VWAP. On the daily Charts I uses 200 sma, 50 sma and 20 sma these days. I believe these moving averages are enough to identify trends and pullbacks etc.

EMA: Exponential Moving Average

SMA: Simple Moving Average

VWAP: Volume Weighted Average Price

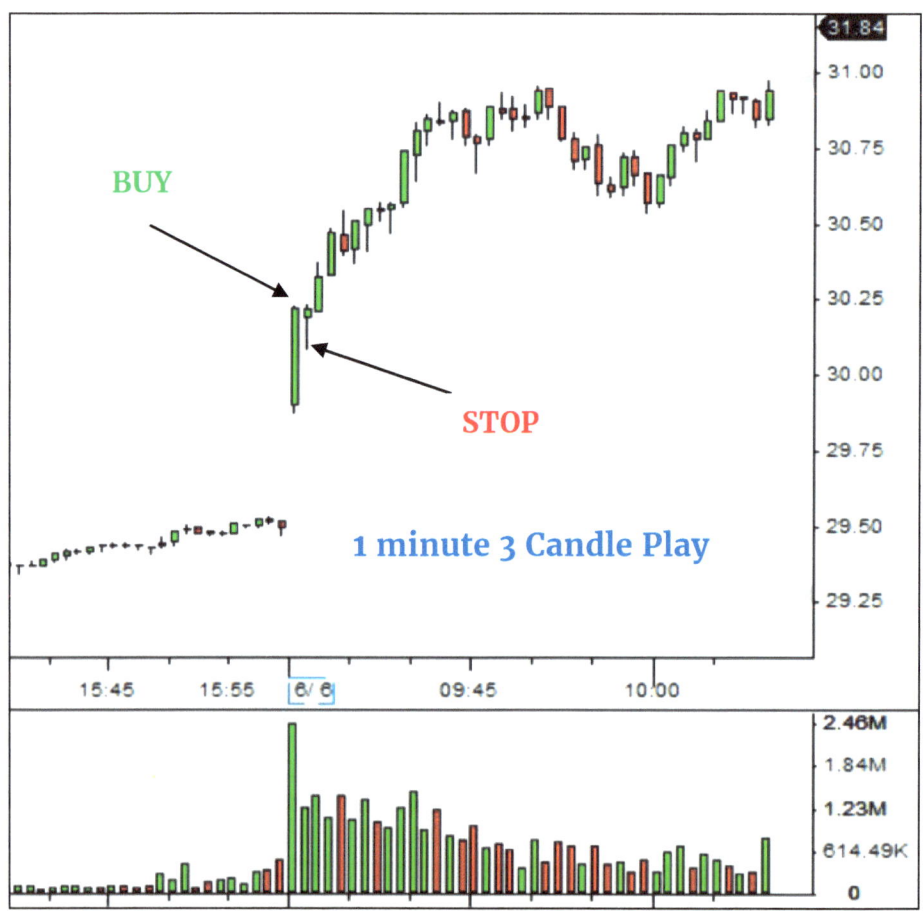

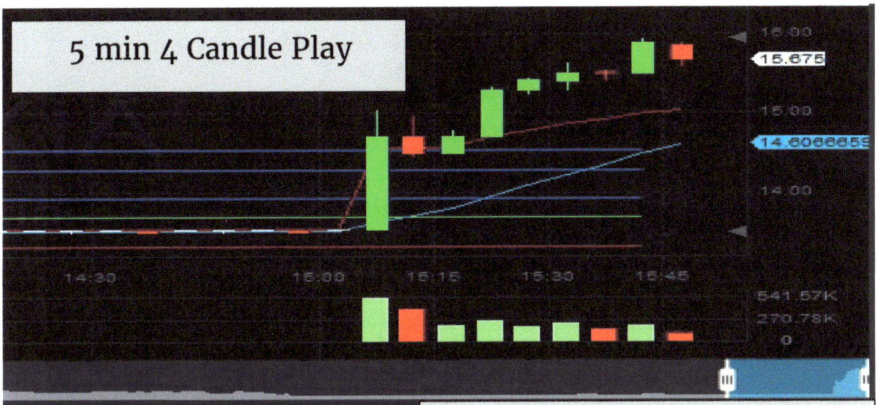

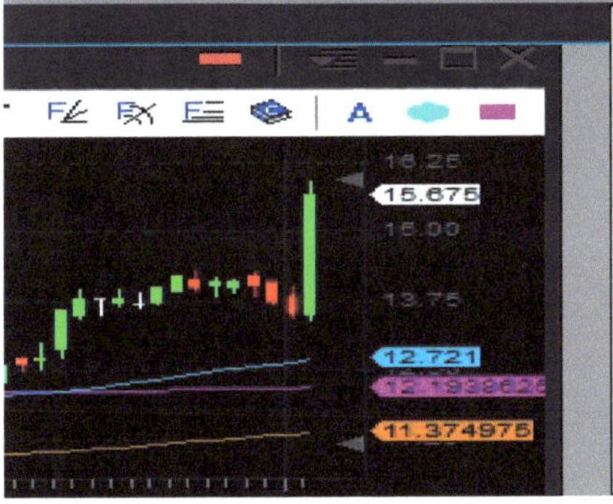

5 min 3 Candle Play

5 min 4 Candle Play

←--- Bullish Daily Chart

As with other high probability plays, a very clear up trading daily is important with room to move.

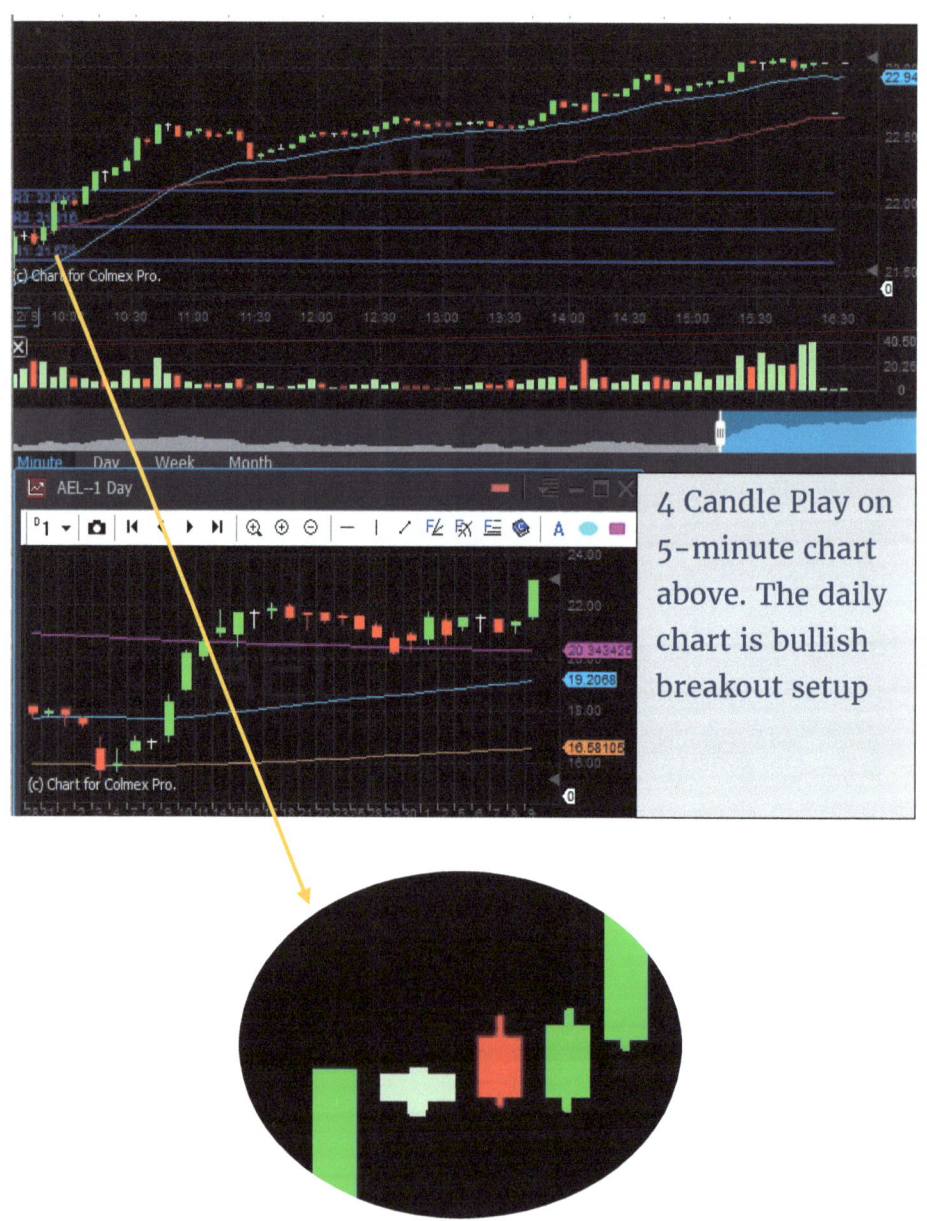

4 Candle Play on 5-minute chart above. The daily chart is bullish breakout setup

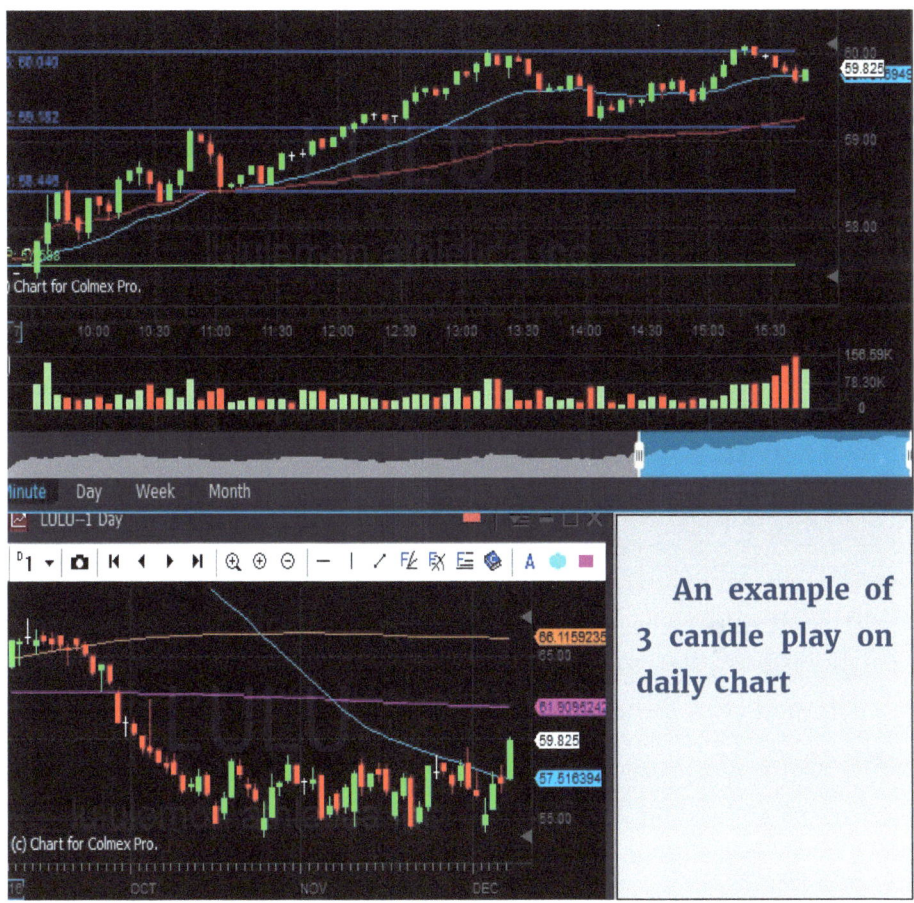

An example of 3 candle play on daily chart

The horizontal lines in the upper intraday chart are called pivot points. I use pivot points to determine exit points or price targets as many computer algos follow them

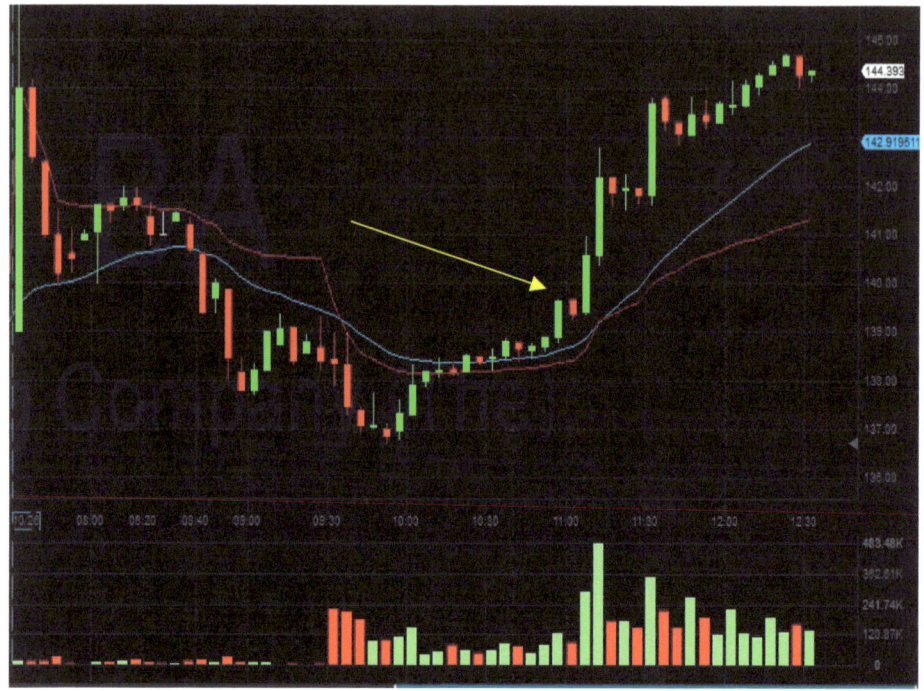

3 Candle Play

Can be used in bottom hunting, in the above chart BA sold hard pre-market and for first 30 minutes. The first retracement was not just a pullback, trend reversal was confirmed by 3 Candle play

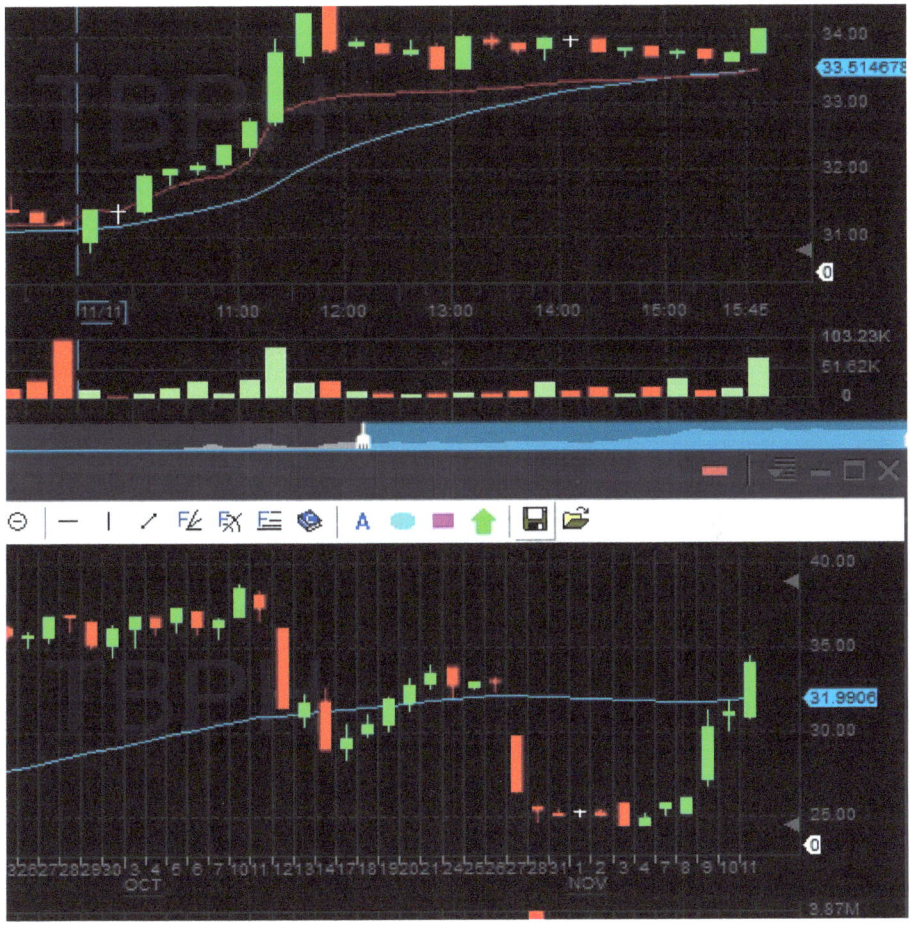

3 Candle Play on both daily chart and intraday 5 minute chart.

I am sure you will be observing top daily gainers/losers every day, they all have a very clear intraday pattern at the beginning of the day

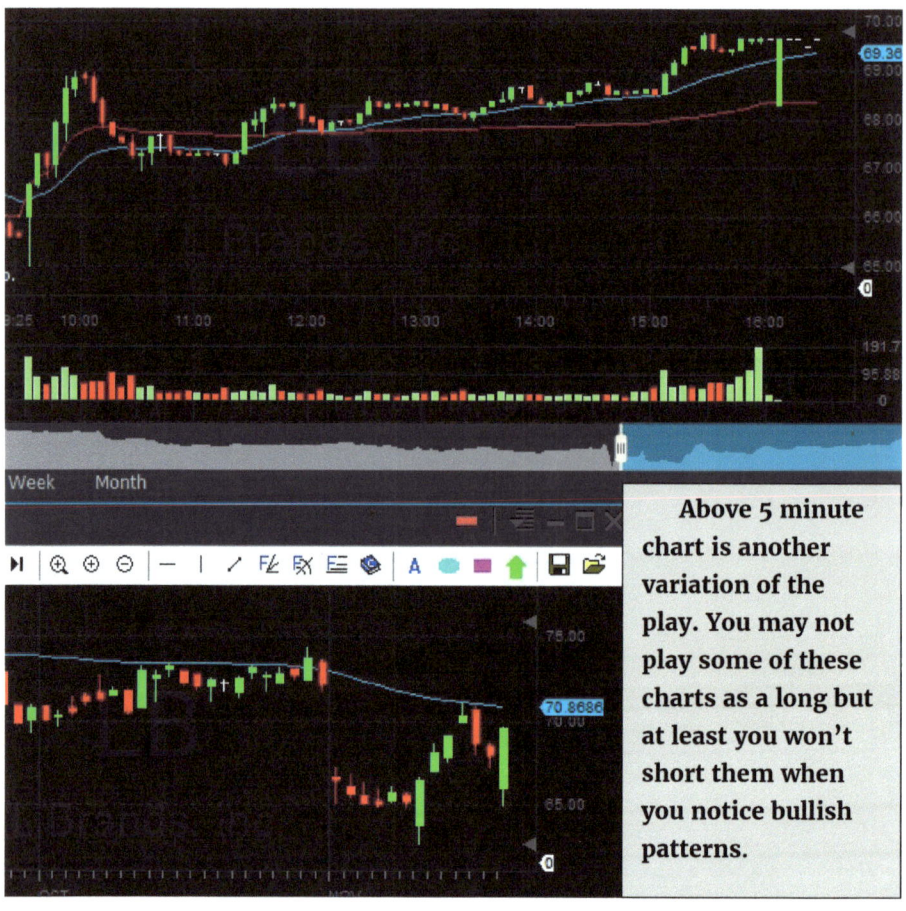

Above 5 minute chart is another variation of the play. You may not play some of these charts as a long but at least you won't short them when you notice bullish patterns.

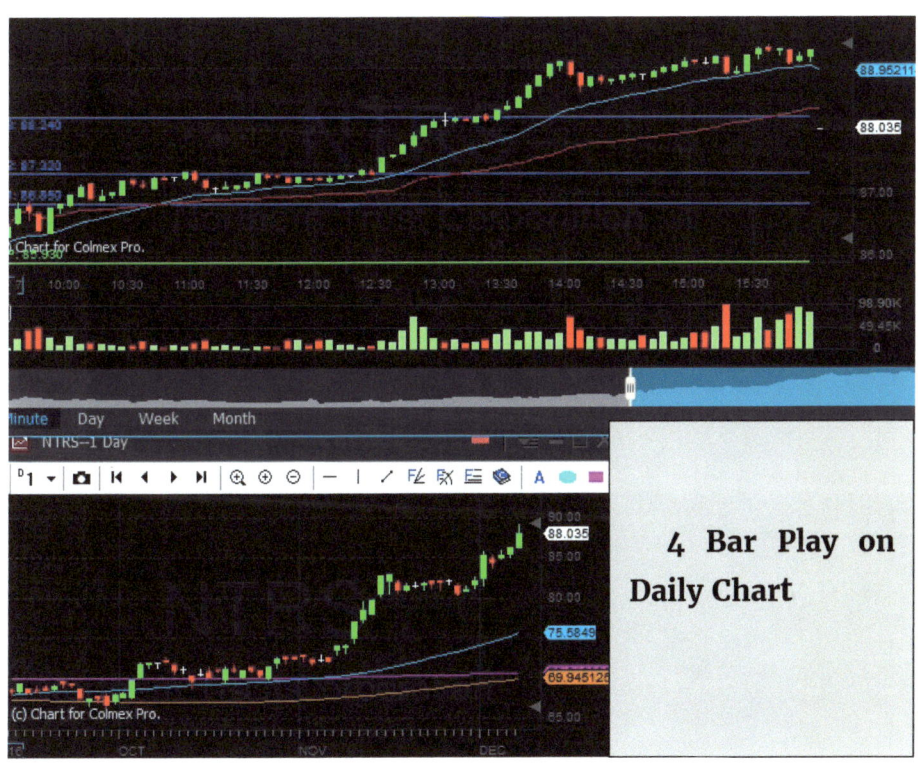

4 Bar Play on Daily Chart

EVERYTHING YOU NEED TO KNOW
IS RIGHT THERE IN FRONT OF YOU.
- JESSE LIVERMORE

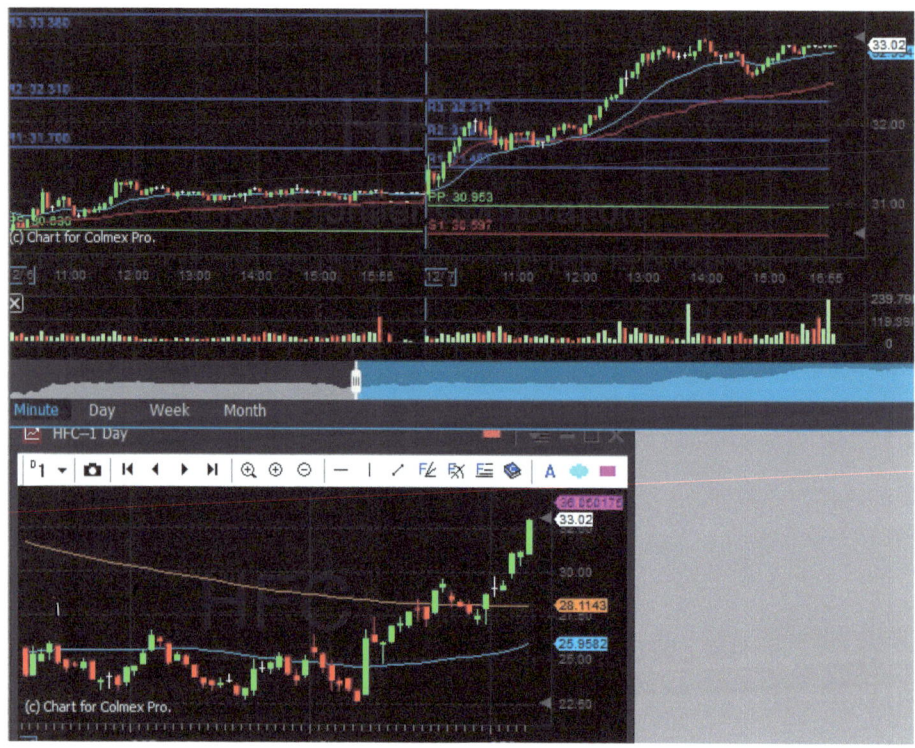

3 Candle Play on Daily, the intraday Play is 4 Candle. In the coming sections I will explain how to find daily 3 Candle Plays

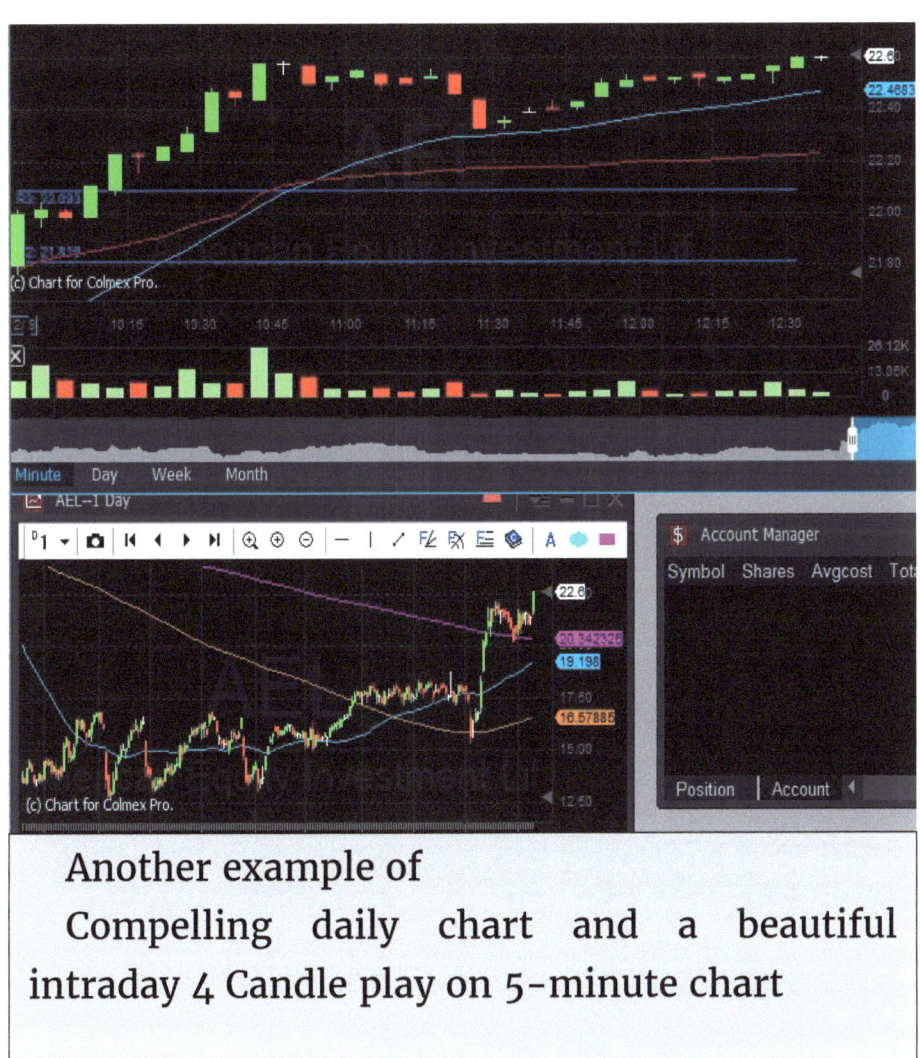

Another example of

Compelling daily chart and a beautiful intraday 4 Candle play on 5-minute chart

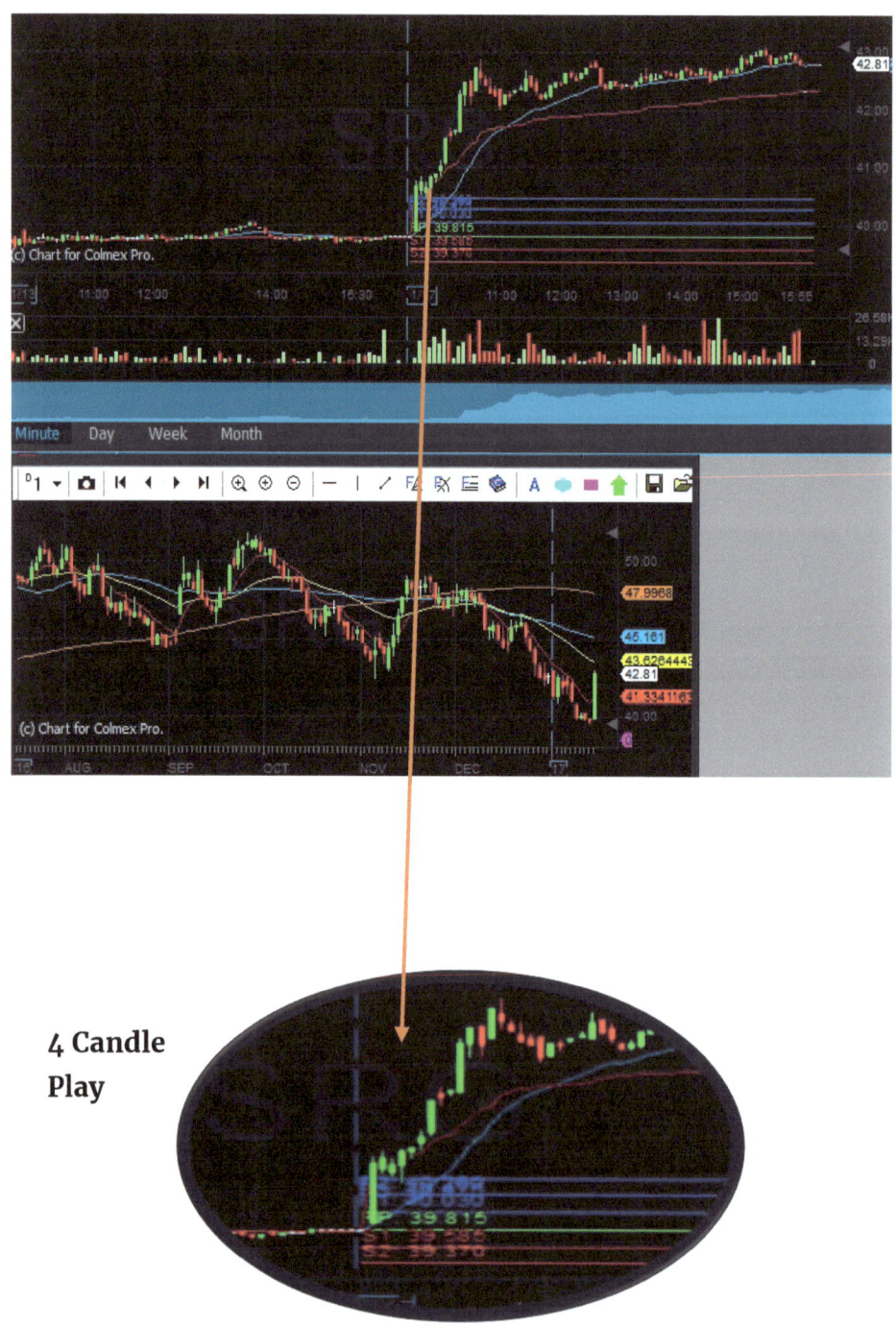

4 Candle Play

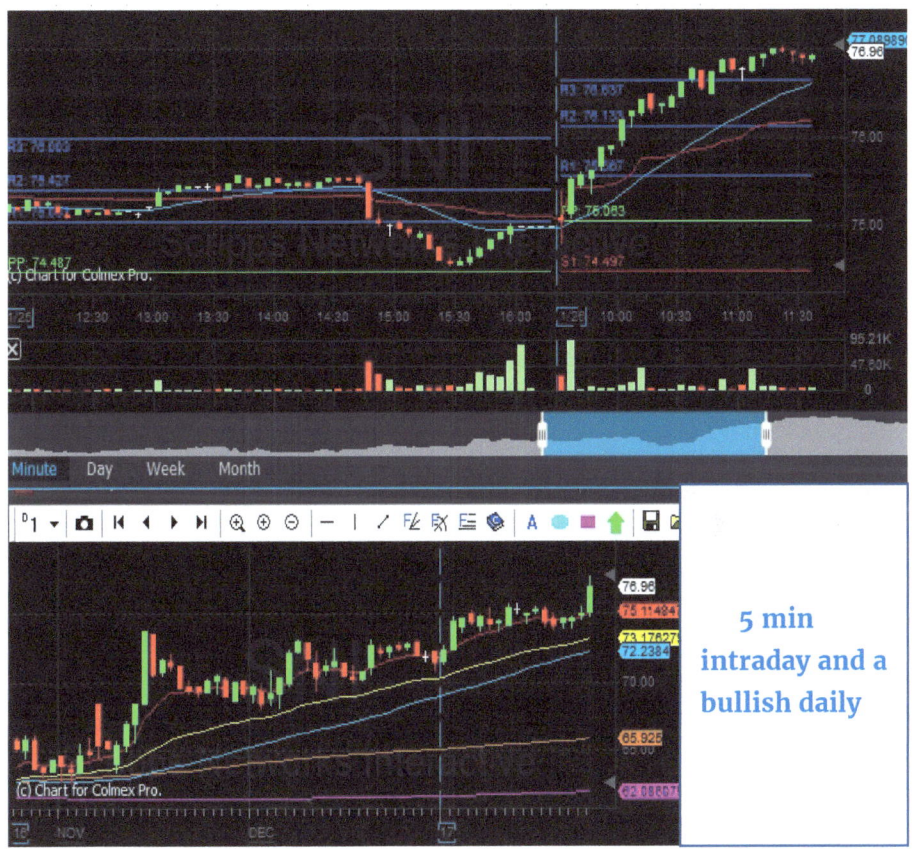

5 min intraday and a bullish daily

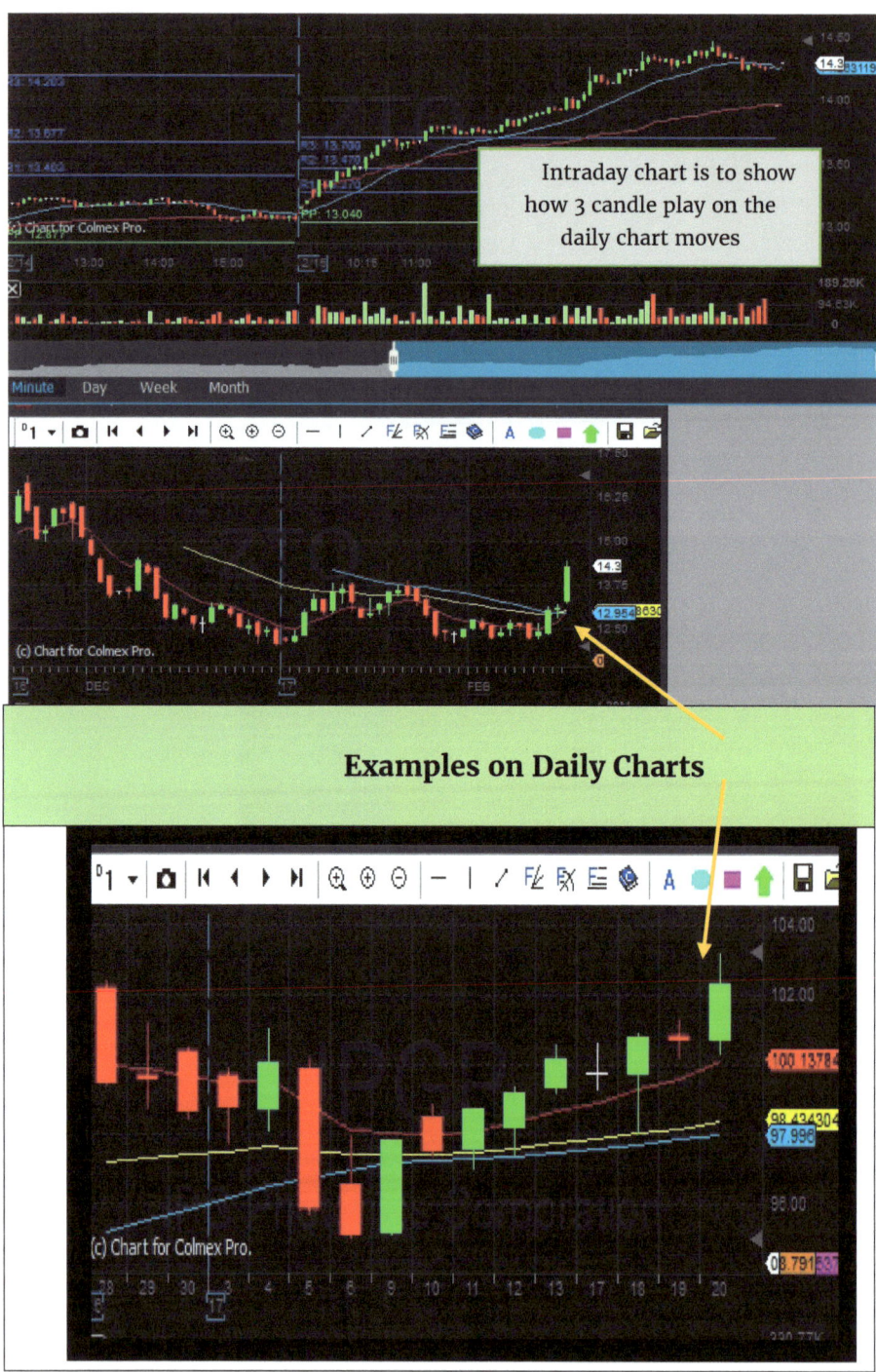

Intraday chart is to show how 3 candle play on the daily chart moves

Examples on Daily Charts

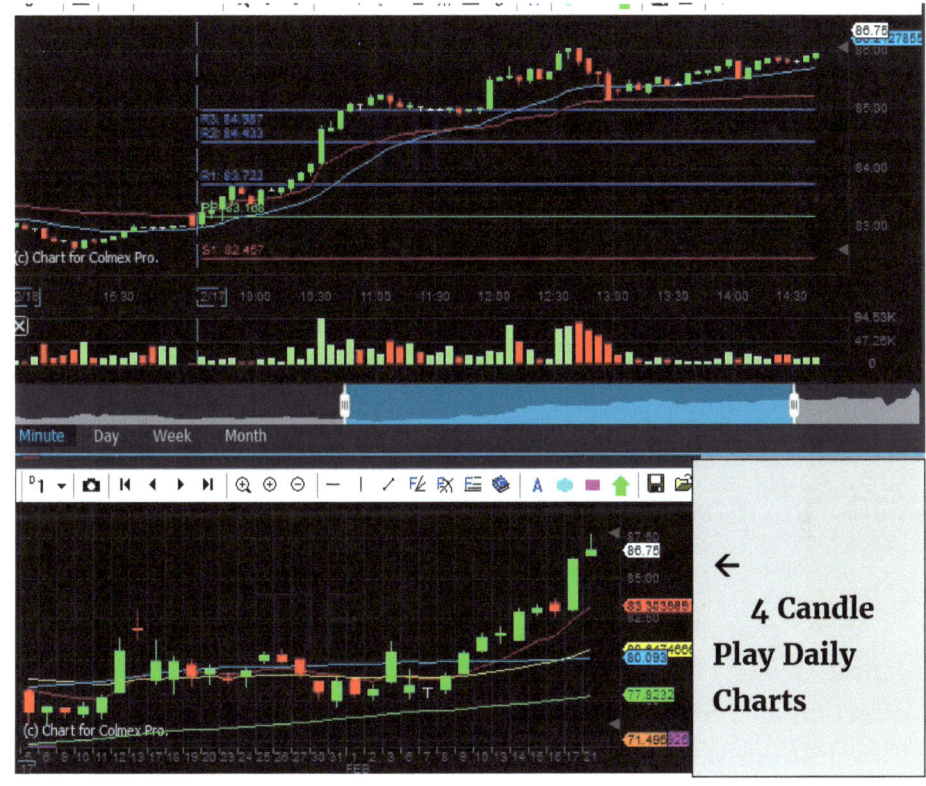

4 Candle Play Daily Charts

I like the fact that 3 candle and 4 candle plays have very tight stop compared to the reward. All these patterns are taken from real markets and I encourage you to open your trading platform and locate these patterns by going back in history of the stocks.

Above chart is an example of Bearish 3 Candle Play. 3 and 4 candle strategy for shorting a stock is exactly the same, except the direction or trend is down. Obviously, the daily time frame should be a clear down trending chart.

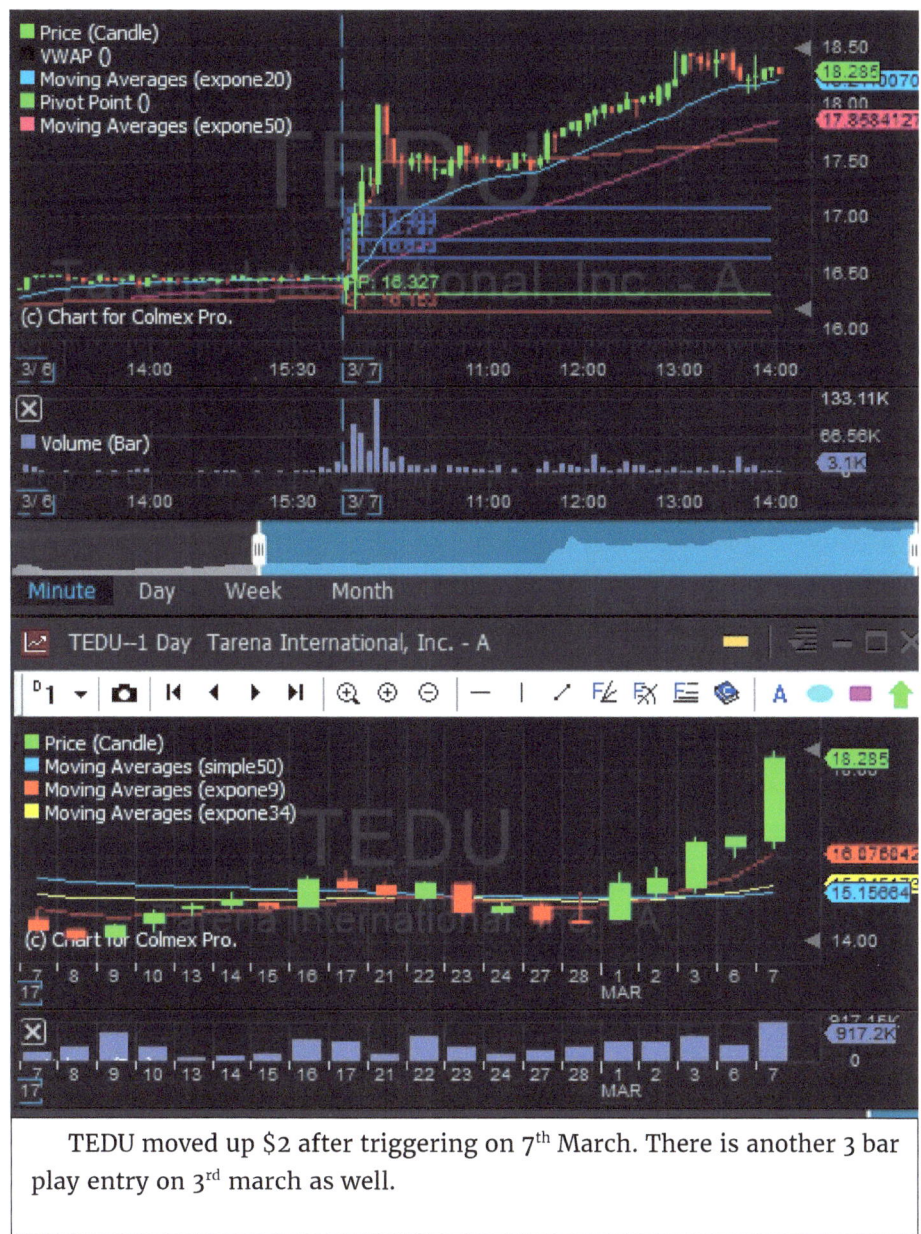

TEDU moved up $2 after triggering on 7th March. There is another 3 bar play entry on 3rd march as well.

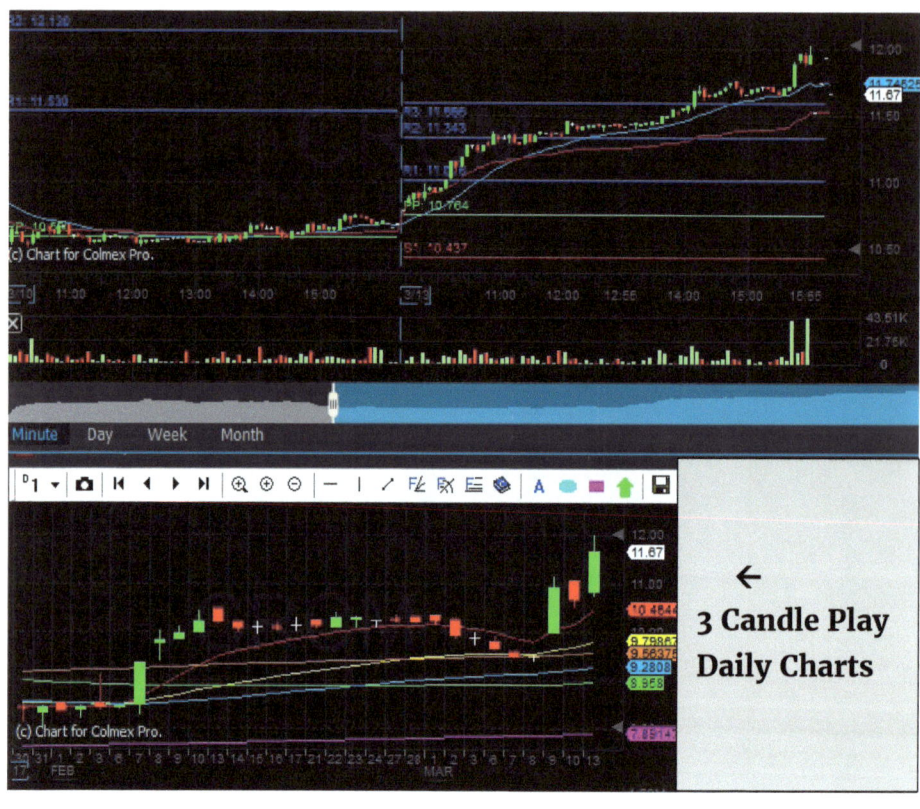

← **3 Candle Play Daily Charts**

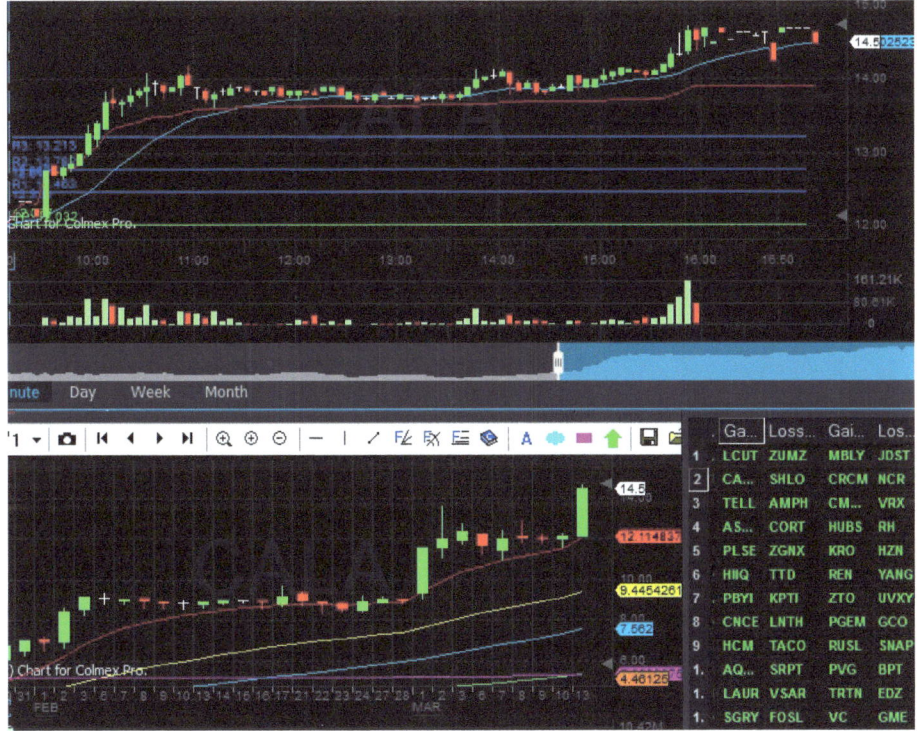

"Every winner needs to master three essential components of trading; a sound individual psychology, a logical trading system and good money management. These essentials are like three legs of a stool – remove one and the stool will fall, together with the person who sits on it."

— Alexander Elder

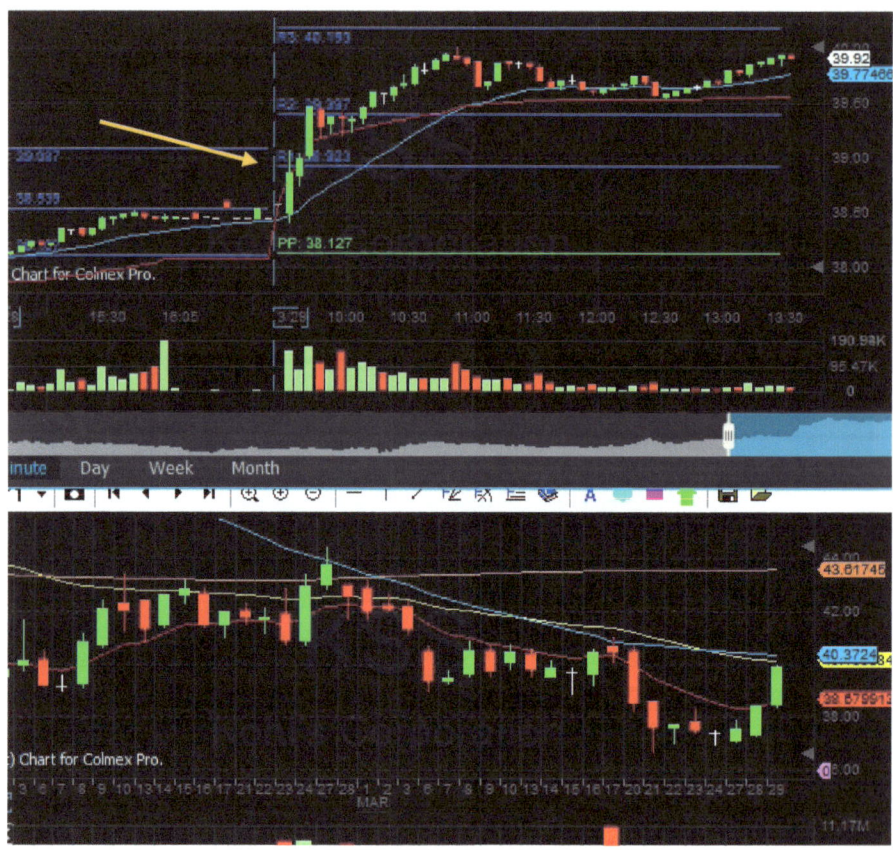

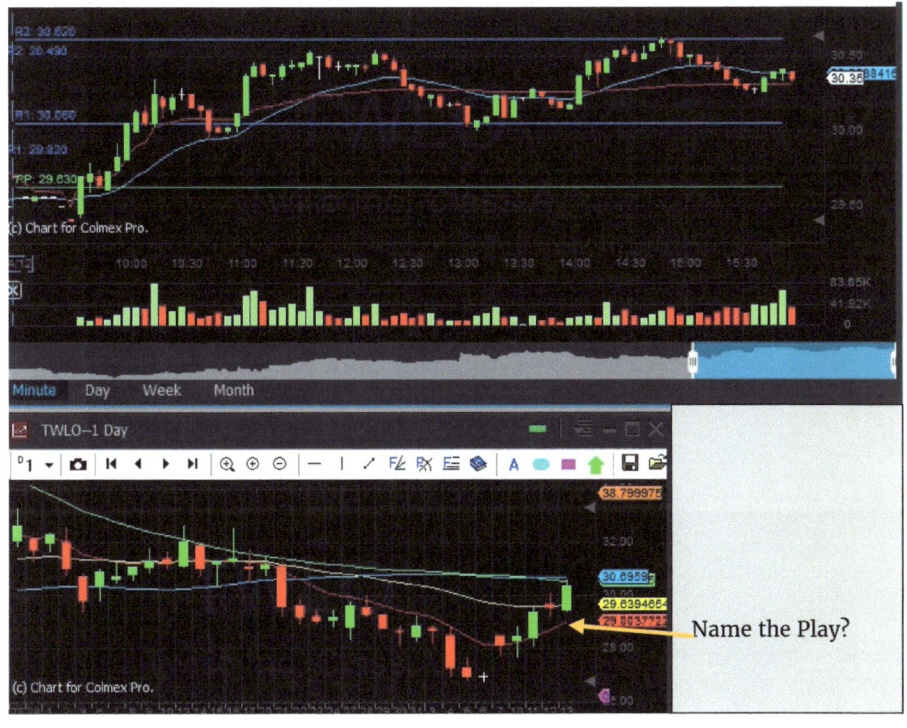

Name the Play?

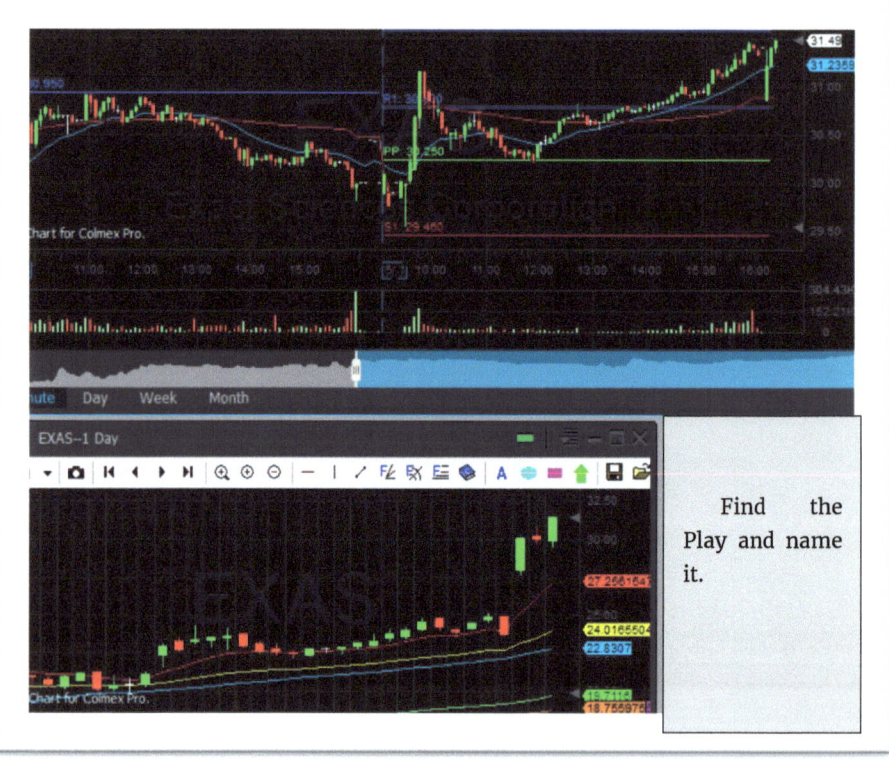

Find the Play and name it.

Most of the charts are taken of Colmex Pro being my broker

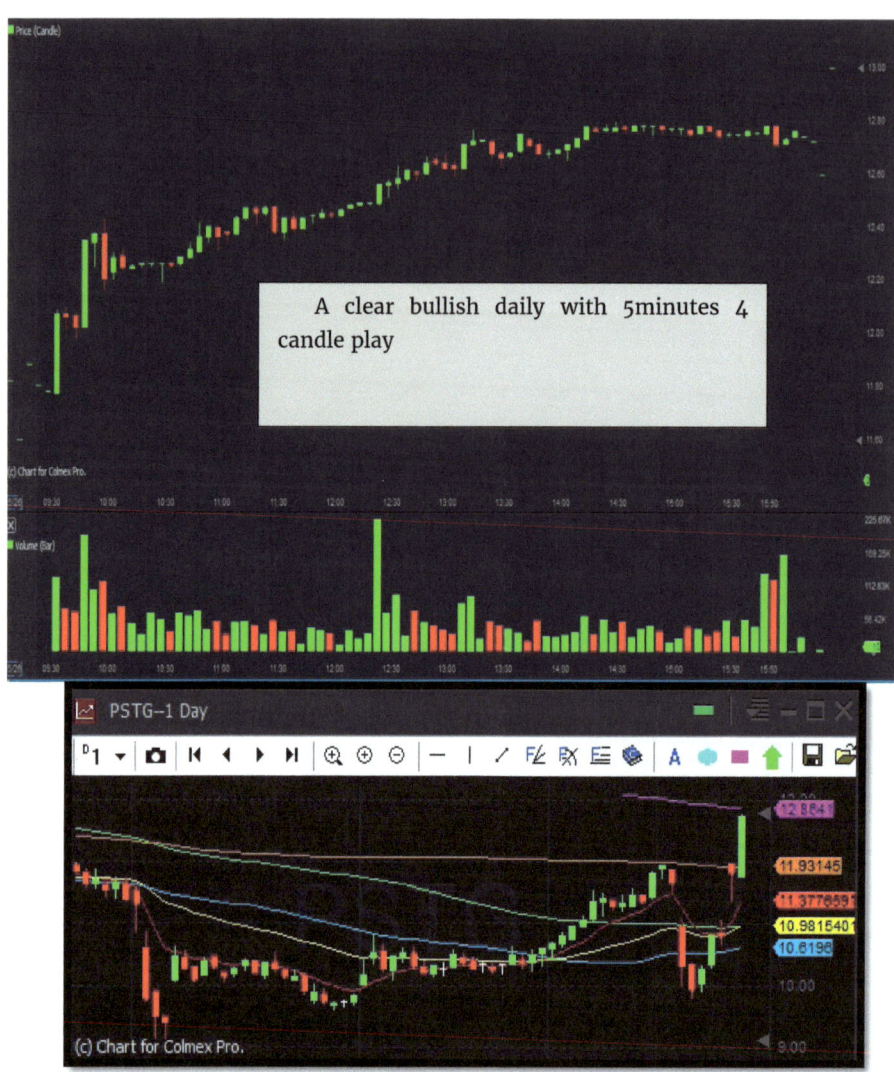

A clear bullish daily with 5minutes 4 candle play

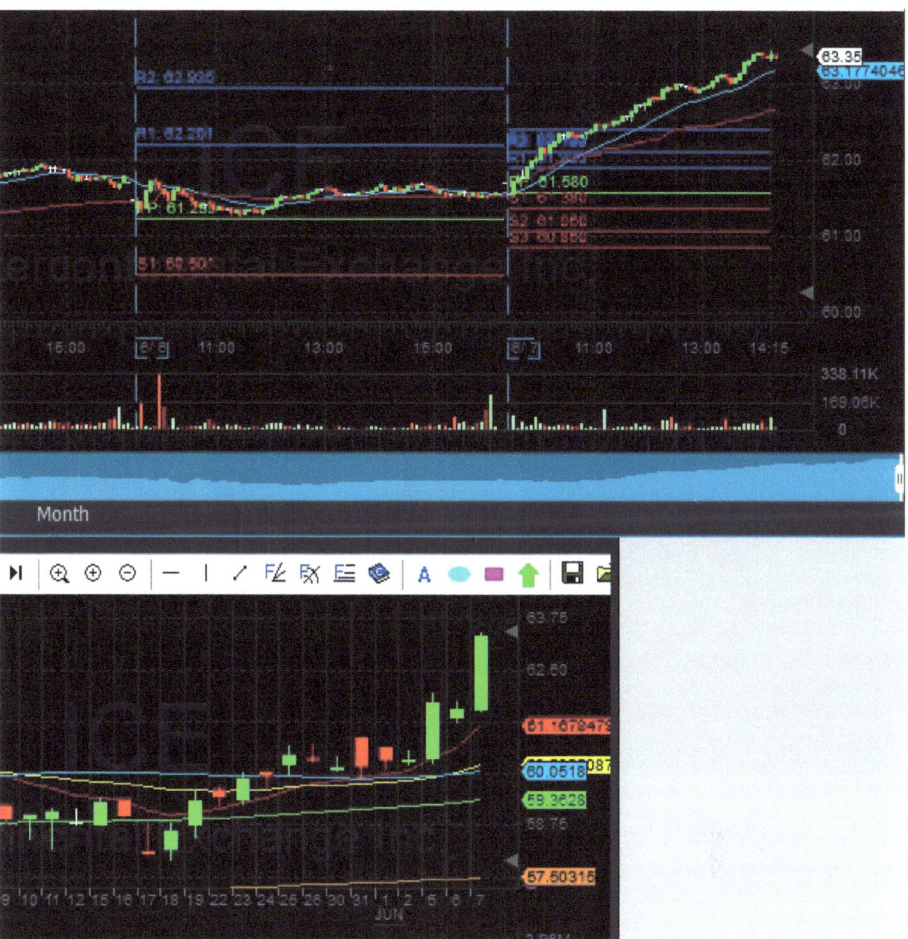

I have added many example charts of intraday and daily charts to show you all possible scenarios of the play. One thing to keep in mind is, 3 candle play and 4 candle play can be seen and play on all famous time frames. I trade this pattern as per the table on page 13.

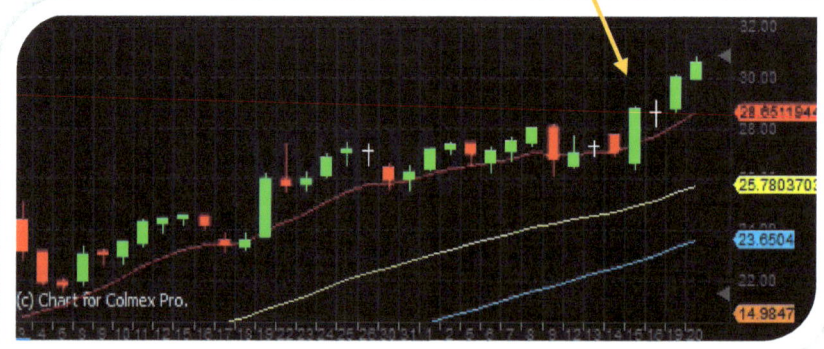

Examples of daily charts

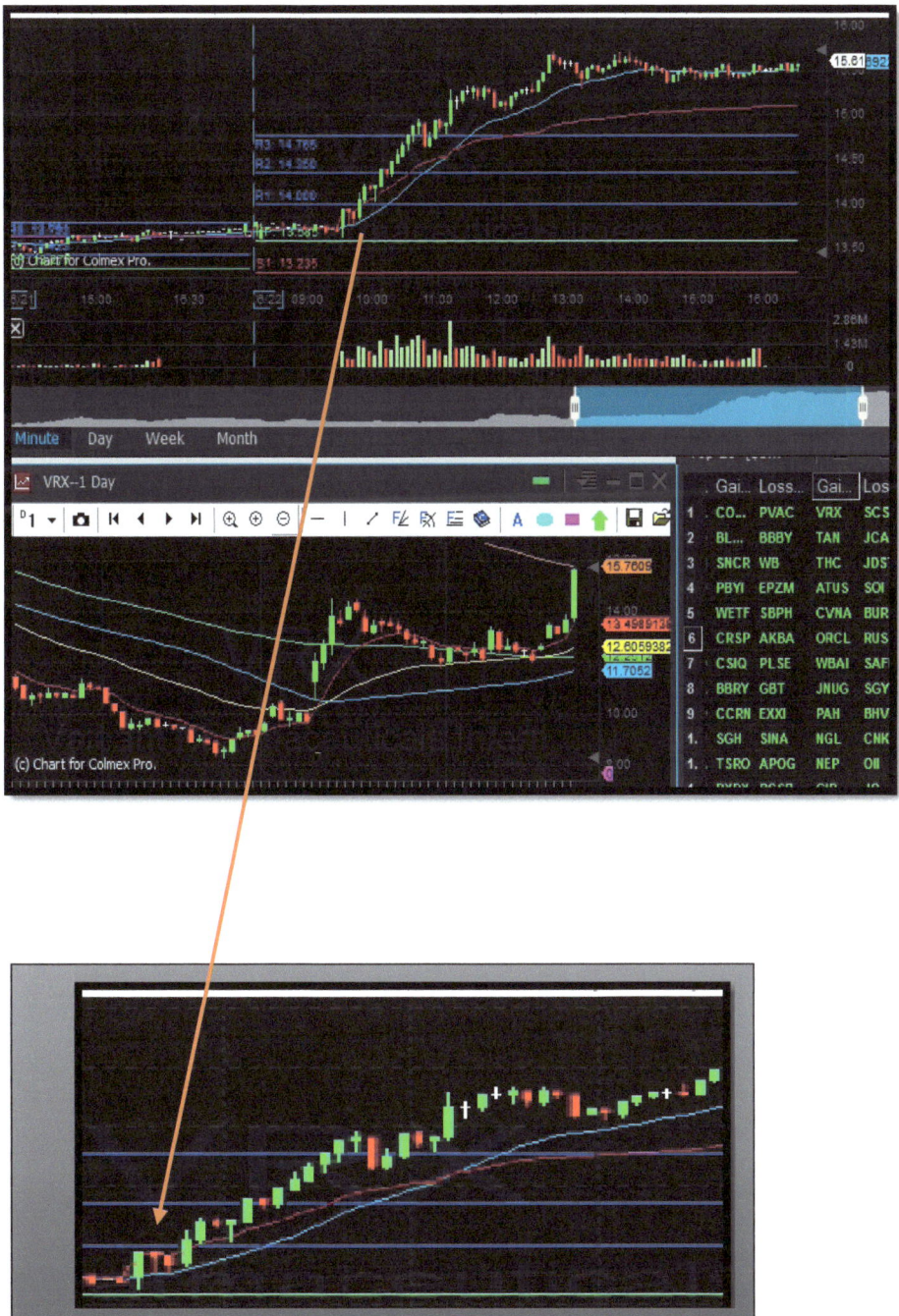

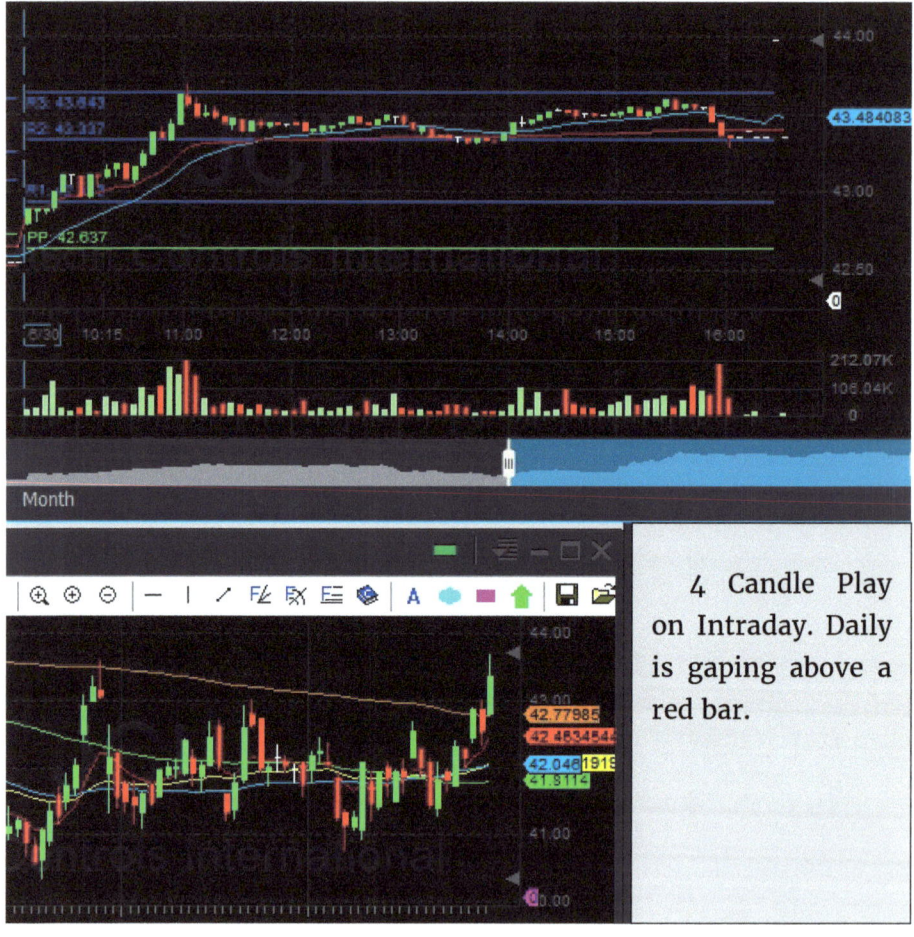

4 Candle Play on Intraday. Daily is gaping above a red bar.

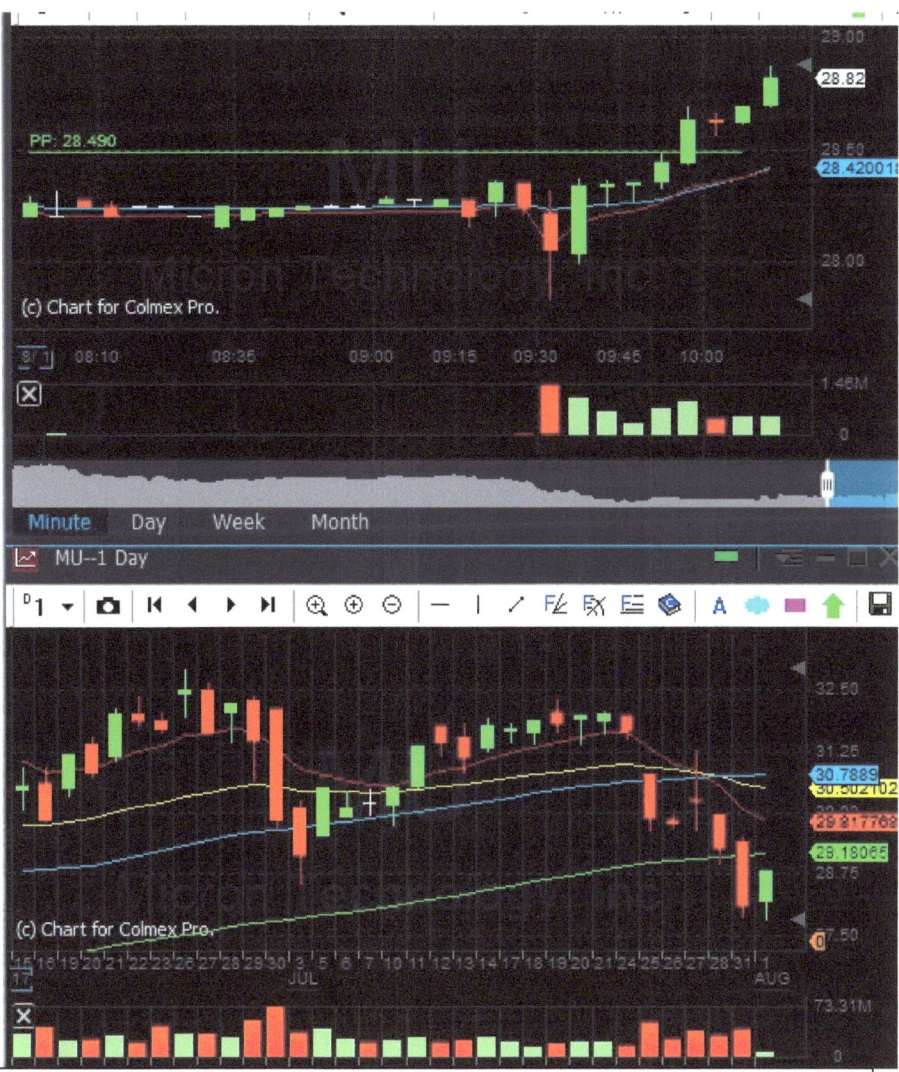

Another example of trend reversal, daily was down a few days, look at the intraday chart on the reversal day, magic isn't it. (ignore the premarket data, market opens at 0930 am)

(c) Chart for Colmex Pro.
SEP
OCT
(c) Chart for Colmex Pro.
TEVA–2 Minute
TEVA–5 Minute

(c) Chart for Colmex Pro.
MAR APR MAY JUN JUL AUG SEP OCT
Minute Day Week Month
EHIC–5 Minute
(c) Chart for Colmex Pro.
(c) Chart for Colmex Pro.

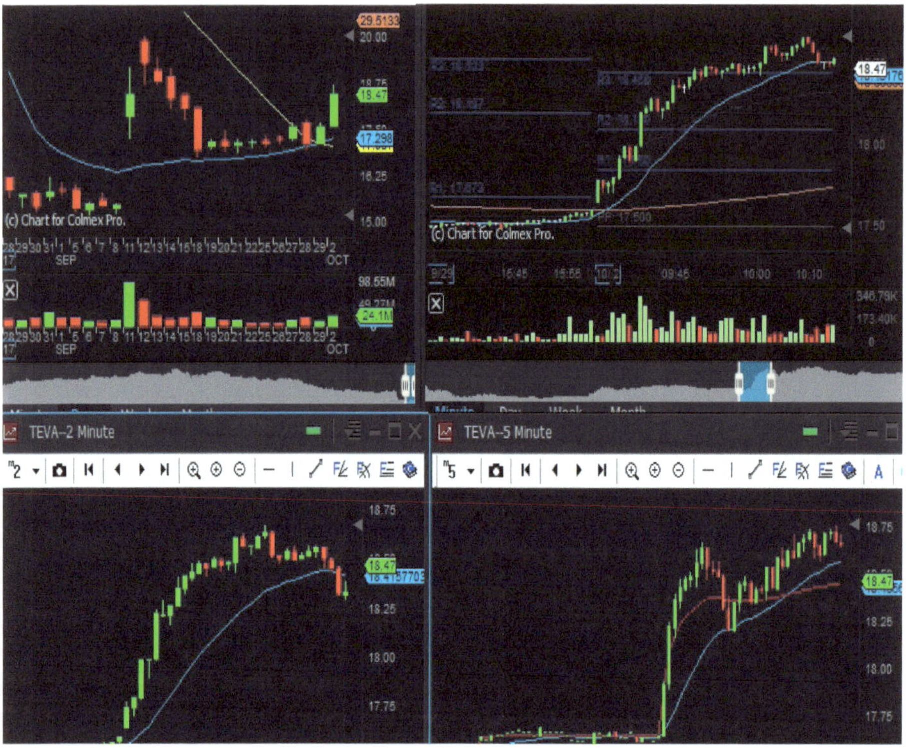

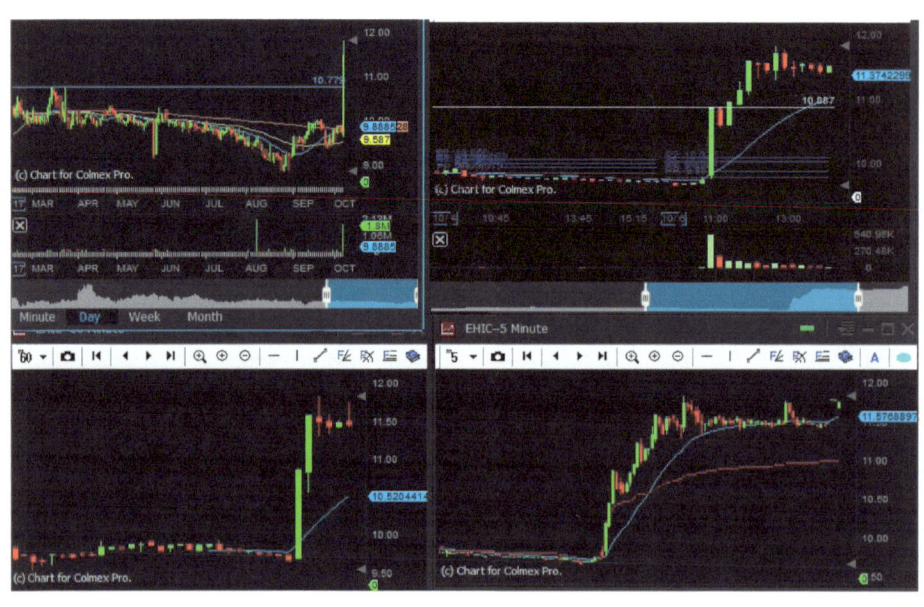

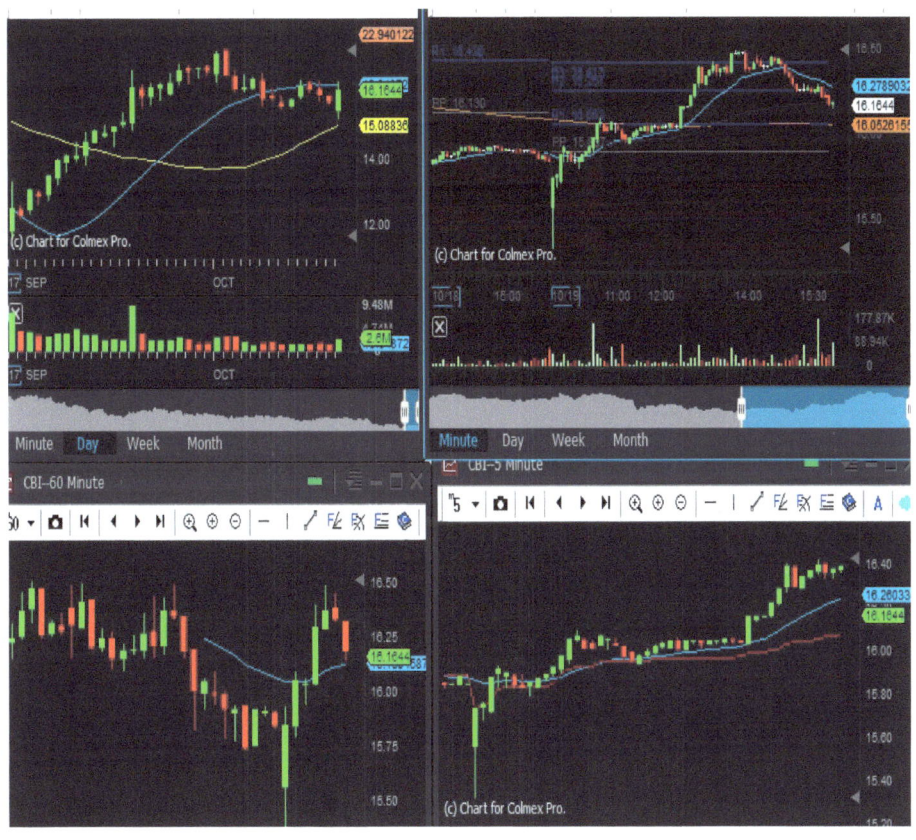

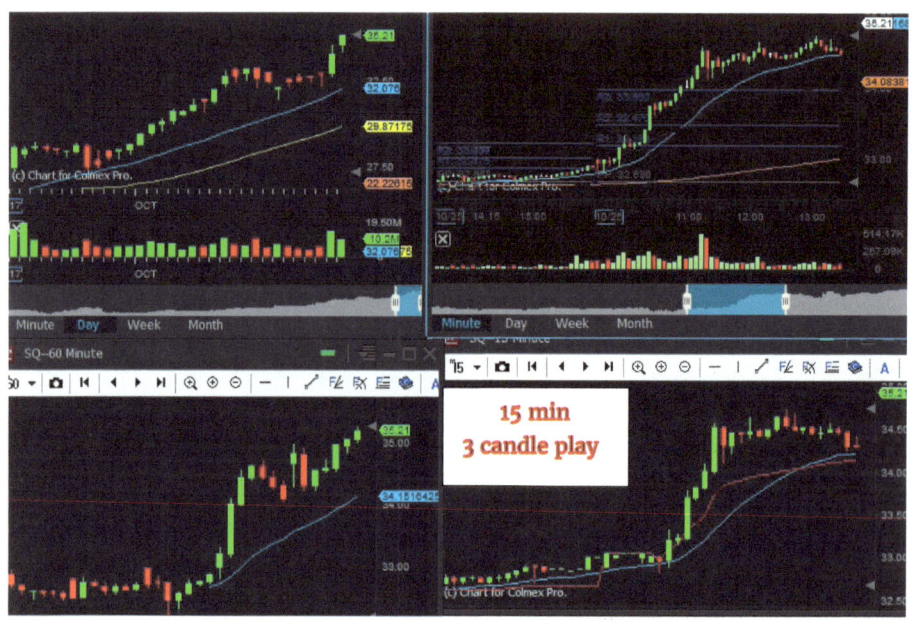

15 min
3 candle play

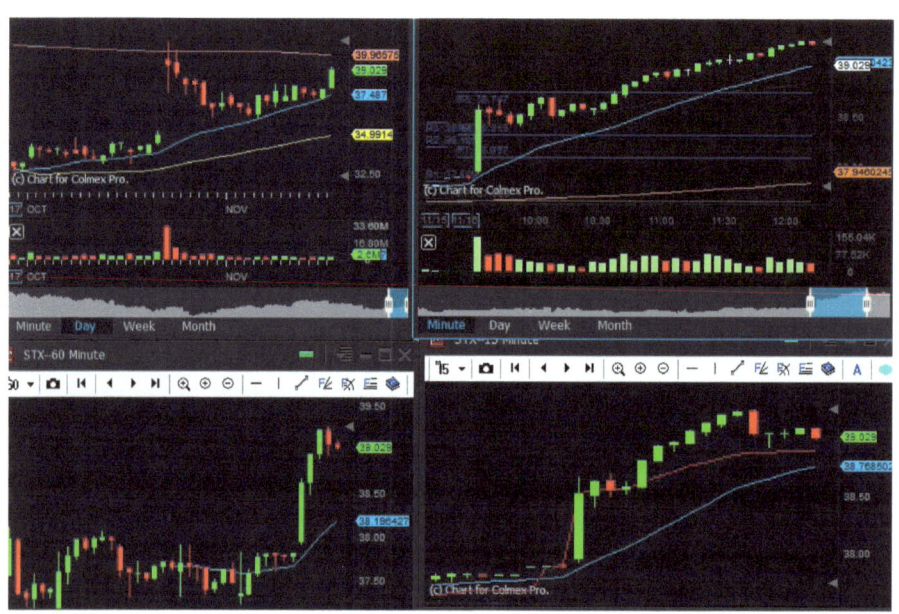

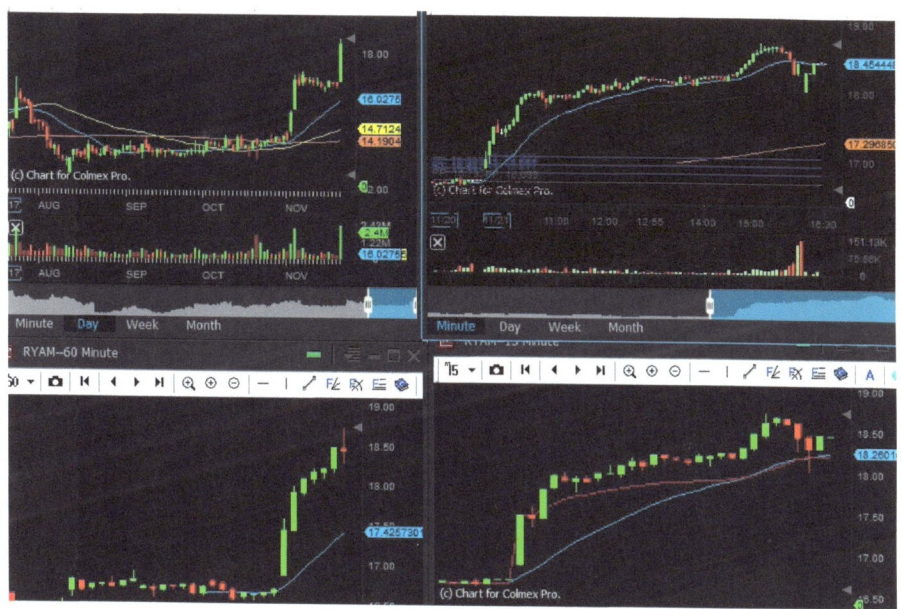

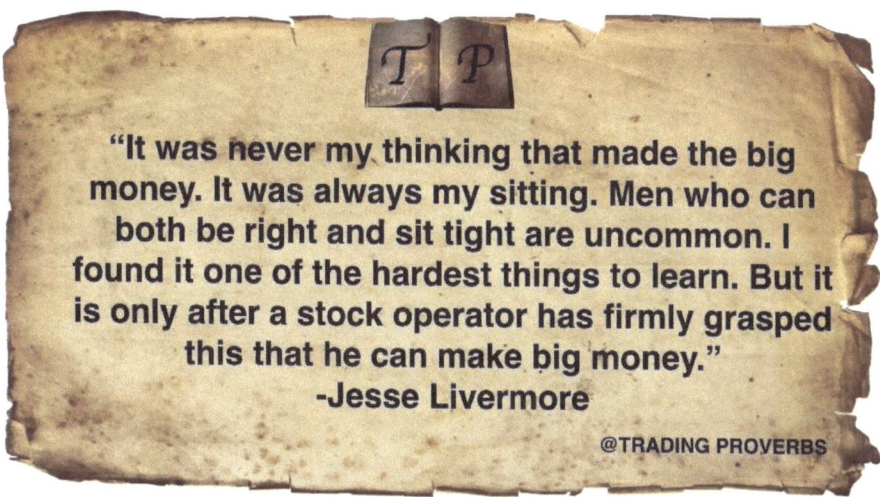

"It was never my thinking that made the big money. It was always my sitting. Men who can both be right and sit tight are uncommon. I found it one of the hardest things to learn. But it is only after a stock operator has firmly grasped this that he can make big money."
-Jesse Livermore

@TRADING PROVERBS

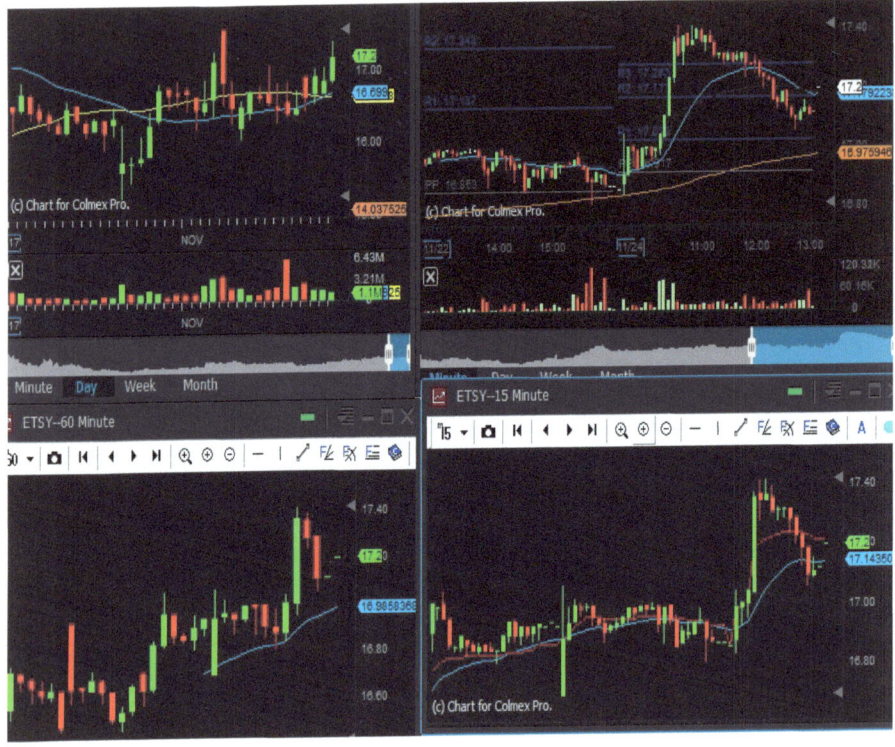

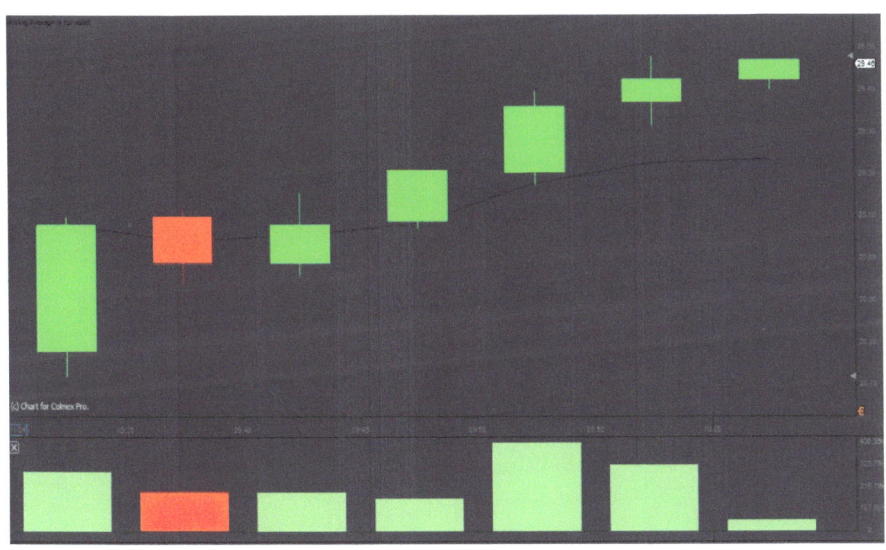

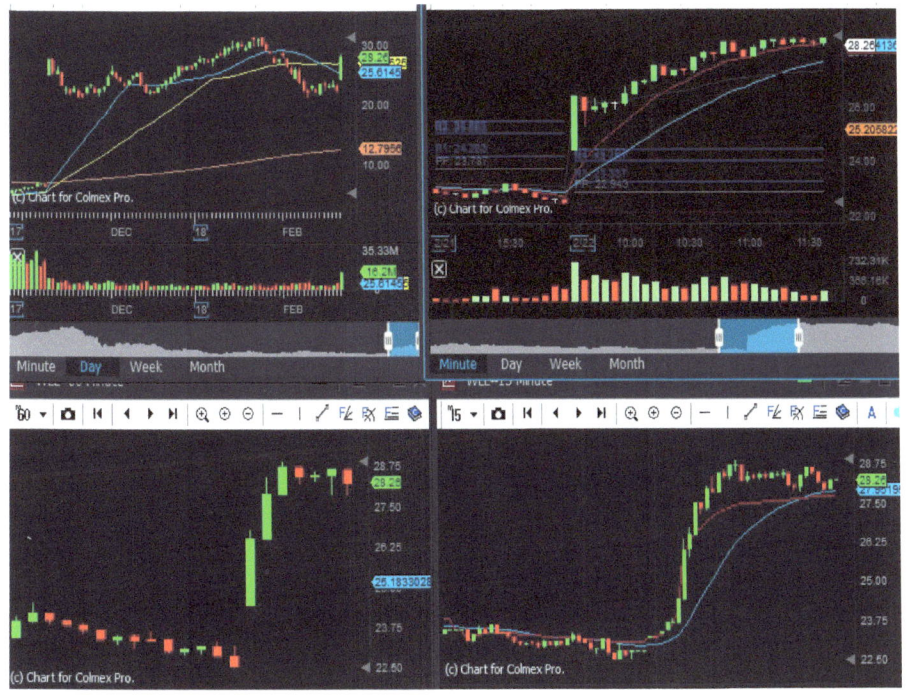

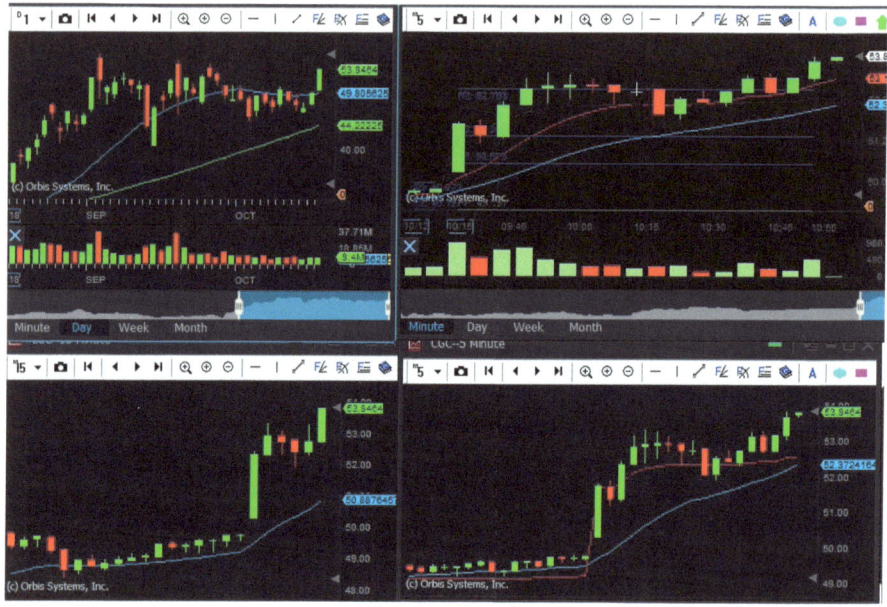

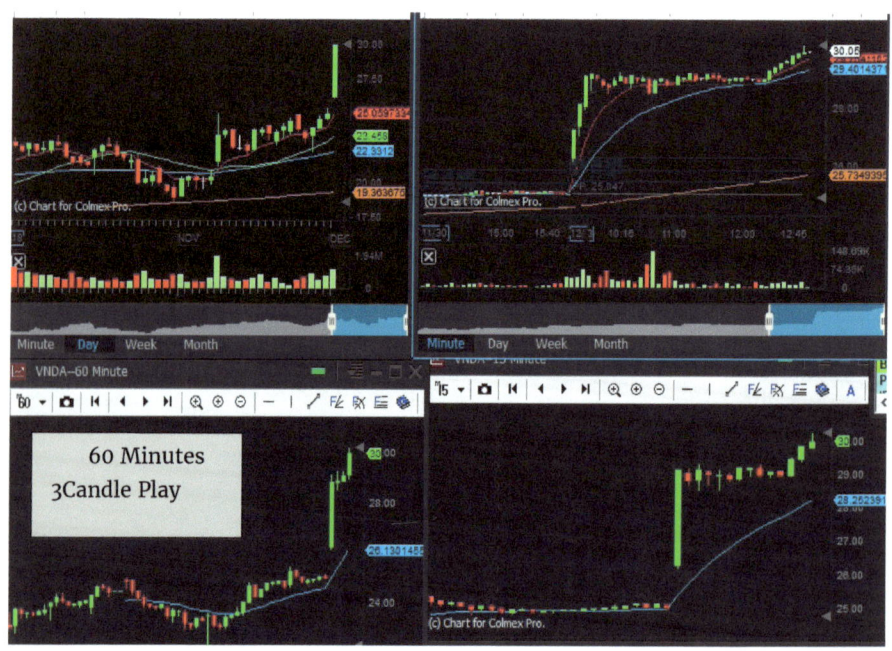

60 Minutes
3Candle Play

Here is another example of using 3 candle play for shorting stocks.

Above is an example of bearish stock. An event on daily chart gives a clear 3 candle play on 5min time frame.

Scanning for the pattern

1- FINVIZ.COM

select Price >5, Current Volume >750KV, Sort as per change, click Charts, candle and daily. You should see the charts of all gainers or looser. Go through these charts every day end of the market and you will learn a lot. Play a bit more with Finviz screen and select DOJI in the Candlestick, this should show you the 3 candle plays. Also I just go through a few hundred charts and find the ¾ Candle plays on daily.

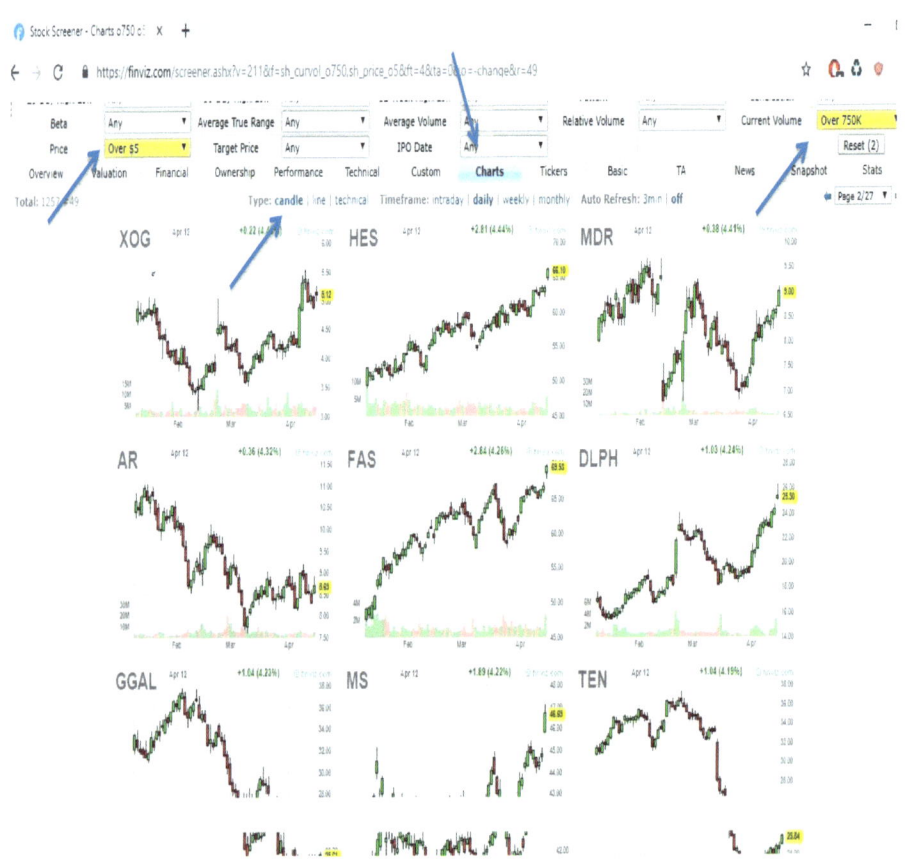

2- Trading platform

Almost all good trading platform provide options for selecting top gainers and losers (stocks). Link your charts to the top gainer and loser list and navigate the list quickly using up and down arrow if your platform allows, else click on each symbol to view same symbol on multiple time frame, as shown in the picture.

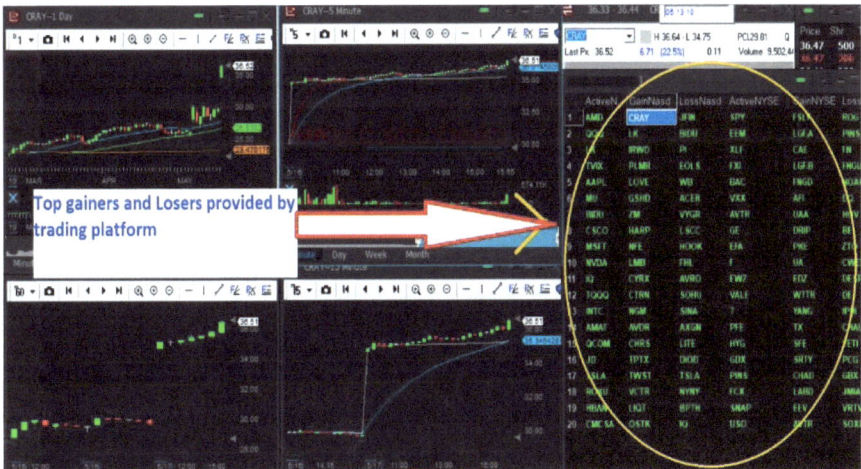

Once you find the charts meeting most of your criteria, you can save them to a watchlist and continue to monitor those symbols for trade entries.

Ending Notes

Many thanks for downloading this book.

Hope you have enjoyed reading and learning this strategy. This strategy should help you recognize the opportunities and act without any emotion of fear, greed or missing out when buying or selling stocks. I have added one chart for shorting, you can re-use the same strategy laid out in this book to short a stock or I will write another strategy book for shorting stocks via this strategy with more example charts (the price would be way less than this book).

Also, I am trying to write ten long and ten shorting strategy books to help break the cost down for those passionate about learning and developing trading skills. Learning one strategy at a time, practicing that strategy, then doing the same with the other strategies is a way to conquer the stock market.

Also, if you need help with this strategy or you have other questions regarding stock market, you are more than welcome to reach out on Facebook etc.

Love, before I say good luck, I would like to request you to leave a review to this book.

Also I have another great book on Breakouts and Break downs, If you are interested to learn more strategies Click here or search How to trade Breakouts and Breakdown, The professional way.

Have a healthy, wealthy and long life.

www.ingramcontent.com/pod-product-compliance
Lightning Source LLC
Chambersburg PA
CBHW041108180526
45172CB00001B/166